Questions and Answers

Q&A

GERMAN
KEY STAGE 4

Keith Tomlins

Principal Examiner

SERIES EDITOR: BOB McDUELL

Letts
EDUCATIONAL

Contents

HOW TO USE THIS BOOK	1
GCSE GERMAN: WHAT DO I HAVE TO KNOW?	1

1 SPEAKING	Revision summary	4
	Foundation Role Plays	9
	Foundation and Higher Role Plays	10
	Higher Role Plays	12
	Narrator Role Plays	12
	General conversation	14
	Presentation	15
	Discussion	16

2 LISTENING	Revision summary	17
	Foundation questions	21
	Foundation and Higher questions	25
	Higher questions	27

3 READING	Revision summary	29
	Foundation tasks	32
	Foundation and Higher tasks	37
	Higher tasks	41

4 WRITING	Revision summary	49
Part 1:	Foundation sample questions and answers	52
	Foundation and Higher sample questions and answers	54
	Higher sample questions and answers	56
Part 2:	Foundation examination practice	57
	Foundation and Higher examination practice	59
	Higher examination practice	61

5 MOCK EXAMINATION PAPER	64

ANSWERS	70

Introduction

HOW TO USE THIS BOOK

The aim of this book is to provide you, the student, with the help you need to reach the highest level of achievement possible in one of your most important examinations – the General Certificate of Secondary Education (GCSE). The book is designed to help all students, up to and including A* grade at GCSE.

The *Questions and Answers* series is based on the belief that experienced examiners can provide, through examination questions, sample answers and advice, the help a student needs to secure success.

Students often find it useful to plan their revision according to some predetermined pattern, during which weaknesses can be identified and eliminated so that confidence can grow. The primary consideration has been to present the main principles on which study can be based.

The *Questions and Answers* format is designed to provide:

- A section on each of the four skills – Speaking, Listening, Reading, and Writing – which will be tested in examination papers. These skills are called **Assessment Objectives**. The brief notes under this heading in each skill section offer you a guide to what exactly is being tested in the examination.

- Easy-to-use **revision summaries** which identify important information which you must understand if progress is to be made in answering examination questions. These summaries will give you vital hints on examination and revision technique. Spend some time on this introduction to each section before tackling any questions and refer back to it whenever you find it necessary.

- Many examples of **examination questions** from actual examination papers. You will be able to improve your own answers by studying the wide range of questions on different types of task together with the examiner's advice on how to approach them. In the Writing section, you will find one task of each type with a sample answer on which the examiner has written a commentary to show any errors or means of improvement. In the Speaking section, there are some Examiner's tips to read before you carry out the tasks.

- **Answers** to the Listening and Reading tasks with **Examiner's tips** on how to cope with the tasks.

- A **CD** which provides the stimulus material for the Listening tasks in the book, as well as a simulated oral test. Do the Speaking tasks from the book before listening to German native speakers carrying out the same tasks: hearing them will help you improve your own performance. For the oral examination and Listening tasks, the CD icon ( ) in the margin refers you to the relevant track numbers.

GCSE GERMAN: WHAT DO I HAVE TO KNOW?

Assessment objectives

What papers will I take?
In GCSE foreign languages examinations, both Full Course and Short Course, there are two different levels: 1) Foundation and 2) Higher. You will be entered for one of these. However, there is at each level an overlapping section which all candidates will have to take, whether they are Foundation or Higher candidates. For the purposes of this book, this common middle section has been called Foundation and Higher.

Four skills are tested at GCSE, each forming a component of the examination:

        Speaking   Listening   Reading   Writing

All four components carry an equal number of points. On each component, eight points will be awarded. These points will represent the following standard of performance:

Introduction

Foundation

0 points = ungraded	3 points = Grade E
1 point = Grade G	4 points = Grade D
2 points = Grade F	5 points = Grade C

You will not be able to achieve a grade higher than C if you enter at Foundation level.

Higher

4 points = Grade D	7 points = Grade A
5 points = Grade C	8 points = Grade A*
6 points = Grade B	

NOTE: Candidates who narrowly fail to achieve Grade D standard on a Higher level paper will be awarded three points. The common middle section for both levels allows Boards to award Grades C and D at the same standard for all candidates.

This is how points on components, when totalled, are converted to an overall GCSE Subject grade:

0 – 1 points = ungraded	18 – 21 points = Grade C
2 – 5 points = Grade G	22 – 25 points = Grade B
6 – 9 points = Grade F	26 – 29 points = Grade A
10 – 13 points = Grade E	30 – 32 points = Grade A*
14 – 17 points = Grade D	

You will be allowed to enter for a different level for each component. If you have a weak area, say Writing, you might wish to take that at Foundation level, whereas you could sit Higher level in the other three components.

You will see from the grading system that there is no gain in taking the Higher level papers unless you have a realistic chance of obtaining a Grade B or above.

At Higher level, your understanding of written German (Reading) and of spoken German (Listening) will be tested to a greater depth. At the same time, greater accuracy is expected when you communicate in spoken German (Speaking) and in written German (Writing).

Use of dictionaries

Dictionaries are allowed for certain papers, according to your Board's regulations. You will find details in the introduction for each unit of the book.

Therefore, you will need to learn how to use a dictionary effectively. Here are some important guidelines:

- Make sure you can spell English properly to speed up your search for the German equivalent of a word in the English–German section.

- Study the key to the abbreviations in the dictionary. These are used, for instance, to show you whether a word is a noun or a verb. If you confuse different parts of speech (e.g. noun/verb), you will be very inaccurate. The gender and plural of a noun are also important: you need to refer to the key to understand how the dictionary sets these out.

- If two meanings are given for a German word, check the plural if used in your text because in the example of *die Bank*, the plural form will depend on whether the word means 'bank' or 'bench'. Alternatively, check the context to see which meaning is more appropriate.

- If you are looking for a German translation of an English word, make sure that there is not more than one possibility. For instance, the English word 'case' could be *der Fall* (meaning 'example') or *der Koffer* (meaning 'suitcase'). The dictionary will probably give other types of case, such as 'briefcase' (*die Mappe/die Aktentasche*). Knowing which is which is vital.

- Don't translate word for word. A literal translation of 'Don't be long' would be *Sei nicht lang!*, which actually means 'Don't be elongated'. You should say *Beeil dich!* (from the reflexive verb *sich beeilen*). 'To go and fetch' is an idiom (i.e. a set pattern) in English: the German equivalent is NOT *gehen und holen*, but simply *holen*.

Introduction

- For Speaking and Listening (if you are allowed a dictionary – this depends on the Examination Board), you need to know the sound of the words. You can't even look up the German word you have heard if you do not have a fair idea of how it is spelt. For Speaking, if you mispronounce a word you have found in the dictionary, you will probably not be understood. Only the largest dictionaries tend to give you the phonetic transcript of a word to show how it is pronounced. You will not have time to use these in exam conditions owing to the number of pages you have to turn and all the possible translations they give, which are beyond GCSE level. So learn carefully how to say words well before the exam.

Defined Content

Try to obtain a copy of the Defined Content syllabus for the examination for which you will be entered. This will list the German words that you are expected to know for Foundation level up to Grade E, and the grammar and structures needed for all Grades. The Defined Content varies only slightly from one Board to another.

Topics

All Boards have to ensure that their syllabus covers the five areas of experience stipulated for the National Curriculum. You will have been studying these areas since you started to learn German. They are:

A Everyday activities
B Personal and social life
C The world around us
D The world of work
E The international world

NOTE: Short Course candidates are tested only on areas of experience B and D.

Although every Board must cover a similar range of topics, these may be grouped under different headings in the Board's syllabus.

For the sake of convenience, you will find below a list of topics covered. Check that you have learned how to understand people speaking and writing in German about the following topics, and that you can speak and write about them in German yourself:

- Personal identification
- Family, friends and social interaction
- House and home, and daily routine
- Hobbies, free time, sport and entertainment
- Geographical surroundings – town and country, and the environment
- Weather
- School and Further/Higher education
- Work, including work experience, part-time jobs, and future plans
- Shopping
- Food and drink – meals at home and eating out
- Travel – public and private transport
- Holidays – including accommodation (hotels, youth hostels etc.), tourism and life in other countries
- Health and welfare – fitness, illness, emergencies
- Services – bank, post office, police, lost property office

1 Speaking

REVISION SUMMARY

ASSESSMENT OBJECTIVES

In the GCSE Speaking examination, you will take either Foundation level (Grades C/D/E/F/G) OR Higher level (Grades A*/A/B/C). You will be tested on your ability to do the following, depending on your level and on the Examination Board for which you are entered, so check your syllabus:

1) Foundation

- Perform a role play, probably involving a transaction, for example in a shop, restaurant or hotel (Tasks A/B/C later in this section of the book).
- Carry out a more complex Role Play with an unexpected question or questions.
- Take part in a conversation related to topics from the syllabus.
- (Dependent on your Board) make a short presentation of a topic chosen by you from those listed in the GCSE syllabus and then discuss it with the examiner.

2) Higher

- Carry out two more complex role plays:
  – the first of these will be the same as set for Foundation level; these Role Plays are called Foundation and Higher in Role Play Tasks D/E/F, in this section of the book.
  – the second will also have some unexpected questions or be based on a situation which is less structured and thus more open-ended (see Higher Task G). Alternatively, some Examination Boards will set a second role play accompanied by pictures (see Higher Task H).
- Sustain a more detailed and complex conversation on a number of topics from the syllabus.
- (Dependent on your Board) make a short presentation of a topic chosen by you from those listed in the GCSE syllabus and then discuss it with the teacher. The standard of the presentation and discussion will, of course, have to be more advanced than that of a Foundation level candidate's.

NOTE: all Boards allow the use of a dictionary during the preparation period before the Speaking test, but not during the test. MEG allows either a monolingual or a bilingual dictionary, whereas all other Boards specify a bilingual dictionary.

EXAMINATION TECHNIQUE

1) Role play: how accurate must you be?

- At Foundation or Foundation and Higher level, the acid test is that a native speaker can clearly understand what you have said. Grammatical errors will be ignored, unless they prevent understanding.
- At Higher level, the more accurate you are, the more your mark will increase.

2) *Du* or *Sie*?

When the person you are supposed to be talking to in a role play (the person whose part is played by your teacher) is somebody you do not know as a friend, for example a shopkeeper, hotel receptionist or a passer-by in the street, you must use the formal German word for 'you' which is *Sie*.

If you are supposed to be talking to a penfriend or exchange partner, then you will use the informal word for 'you' which is *du*.

Speaking

REVISION SUMMARY

3) General Conversation – all levels
If the examiner says something you do not understand, do not sit there in silence, say one of the following:
- *Ich weiß es nicht.*
- *Ich habe es nicht verstanden.*
- *Wiederholen Sie bitte.*
- *Würden Sie bitte langsamer sprechen?*

If the examiner says something with which you are meant to agree, do not just say *Ja*. Follow it up with a sentence to get extra credit. For example:

Spielst du gern Fußball?
Ja, ich spiele jeden Samstag mit meinen Freunden.

If the examiner says something with which you disagree or wish to deny, do not just say *Nein*. For example:

Ißt du gern Fleisch?
Nein, das schmeckt mir nicht. OR
Nein, ich bin Vegetarier(in).

Try to give more than one-word answers generally. The essential requirement is to communicate, to get the whole message across as clearly and as accurately as possible. Extra marks will be available to reward good pronunciation, accuracy, range of vocabulary and structures offered, prompt replies and fluency of speech. For the top language mark at Foundation level, you must talk in the future and past tenses as well as in the present.

4) General Conversation – Higher
Additionally at Higher level you will be rewarded for your ability to express your opinions and feelings, to argue and defend your views, to take the initiative and generally to hold your own in a genuine conversation. For the top mark you would also be expected to be very accurate and to use a wide range of vocabulary, structures and idioms (i.e. typically German ways of saying things).

5) Presentation of a chosen topic
Some hints:
- **Prepare yourself.** Obviously you need to put a lot of preparation into this. You need to make some vital points in your best German and keep to the time limit.
- **Make it interesting.** It is important to make your presentation sound interesting. A series of facts about a topic can be immensely dull. Imagine you are the poor teacher/examiner who may have to hear details of the same topic not only a few times on the same day, but also several days in a row!
- **Be original.** At the very least make sure that what you have to say is different from the material which anyone else at your school or college is going to offer. It is up to the individual to give the subject some originality.
- **Practise.** Practise saying your presentation into a cassette recorder and listen to what you sound like. Pretend you are talking to a group of people in front of you who have come especially to listen to you. You could ask your teacher to record your teaching group with each one of you talking individually to the others during a lesson.
- **Imagine people are listening.** What you must have is a sense of audience. This makes your tone of voice and your whole approach more interesting. On the day of the examination, conquer your nerves. Do not just talk into the microphone. Be aware of your teacher who is present. In the examination room, you must also still imagine that a group of people are sitting there eager to hear what you have to say.

1 Speaking

REVISION SUMMARY

- **Say why you chose the topic.** It helps to state in your Presentation why you chose the topic and to convey a clear interest in it. If it is not just a personal topic, try to tell the examiner why it is of interest or importance to him/her.
- **Cover the important points, but leave the detail until later.** It does help the examiner if you cover the main points which you wish to raise later in the discussion, because s/he will try to deal with these first before mentioning others. However, you should not make a mere list of points.
- **Sound lively.** Above all, the presentation should be lively and capable of capturing and sustaining the examiner's interest. Don't make it sound too rehearsed. You do not want to sound like a well-trained parrot!

ACTIVE SKILLS

For Speaking, as for Writing, you need to develop your active vocabulary and grammar. It is quite easy to remember the meaning of a German word for the purpose of Listening and Reading. To learn how to put something into German is much harder and needs more practice, yet most students unfortunately spend less time on this active skill.

If you do not have a book in which German words are provided with their meanings, then write them down yourself, in a vocabulary book for example, ready to revise them. For Speaking and Writing, cover up the German words and test yourself on translating the English into German. It is better to learn 20 a day early in your course, but if you have started your revision late, you will have to try 50 at a time. It is not helpful to do more at one go, since your brain will not take them in. Take a break, do some other work, and return to the word list later. Grammar should also be studied in small sections or topics at a time.

You should shut your grammar guide and see if you can jot down the main points accurately without help. Unless you can do this, you should re-read that section of grammar and test yourself again, before proceeding to the next topic.

Question words (*wann*, *wo*, *wohin*, *woher*, *was*, *wer*, *warum*, *wie*...?) are helpful for the role play. Can you use them?

Wann fährt der Bus?	When does the bus leave?
Wo ist die Post?	Where is the post office?
Wohin fährst du?	Where are you travelling to?
Woher kommst du?	Where do you come from?
Was spielst du gern?	What do you like playing?
Wer ist dein Freund?	Who is your friend?
Mit wem spielst du?	Who do you play with?
Warum bist du müde?	Why are you tired?

Note especially the use of *wie* and *wieviel*:

Wie ist das Wetter heute?	What is the weather like today?
Wie geht's?	How are you?
Wie kommst du zur Schule?	How do you travel to school?
Wie sieht dein Bruder aus?	What does your brother look like?
Wie viel Geld bekommst du?	How much money do you get?
Wie viele CDs hast du?	How many CDs do you have?

Time expressions are very useful. Revise, for example, days of the week/months/dates/clock times:

am Montag(nachmittag) BUT *montags/montagnachmittags*
am Abend BUT *in der Nacht*
um zwei Uhr/um halb zwei/um Mitternacht/um 12 Uhr mittags

Speaking 1

> *im Sommer/im April*   BUT   *an einem schönen Aprilmorgen*
> *zu Weihnachten/zu Ostern/zu Pfingsten*
> *jeden Tag/letztes Jahr/letzten Monat* (Accusative)
> BUT *eines Tages/eines Morgens* (Genitive – indefinite time)
>
> Some other handy expressions:
>
> *zwei Stunden später*   *nach dem Mittagessen*
> *morgen (ganz) früh* = (early) tomorrow morning
> *am nächsten/folgenden Tag*   *gestern vormittag/abend*
> *drei Stunden lang*   *bis spät in die Nacht*

REVISION SUMMARY

CONFIDENCE IS THE KEY TO SUCCESS

You need to go into the examination room full of confidence. To do this, you need to have had a lot of practice. In addition to the practice which you have had at school, you should have spoken as much German as you can outside it. Some suggestions:

- Speak German to a friend or group of friends preparing the same examination or who have taken it in a previous year.
- Chat with an elder brother or sister or parent who is good at German or who has sat the examination.
- Make the most of any opportunity to visit a German-speaking country to hold conversations with your penfriend (if you have one) or with any other people who are prepared to listen to you.
- Talk to yourself out aloud. Explain to your family why you are doing this, in case they doubt your sanity!
- Record yourself speaking on a cassette recorder and play it back to listen to yourself. You will not feel nervous in the examination room at the thought of your speaking test being recorded, as many candidates are, if you have already made recordings and listened to them.
- Do the Speaking tasks on the CD accompanying this book.

TASKS TO BE PERFORMED ON CD

Listen to the CD and, using the Examiner's tips, try to carry out the Speaking tasks as follows:

1 Do the Foundation, the Foundation and Higher, and the Higher Role Play exercises.

For Role Play Tasks A to G, you will first hear the teacher's question or statement followed by a short tone. You are advised to pause the CD at the tone to give your own answer and then to restart it, once you have answered.

When you have finished doing each entire Role Play Task, you should play it again, not saying anything but listening to the candidate's role as performed by the German speaker.

In Role Play Task H, there are no tones. You should try to tell the story yourself before listening to the German speaker's version.

2 When you feel that you need a change from Role Play, answer the Foundation and the Higher General Conversation questions grouped by topic. Foundation here means the level of grades E/F/G only; Higher means beyond Foundation, in other words grades A*/A/B/C/D. Remember that you will take an Oral Test aimed either at grades A*/A/B/C or grades C/D/E/F/G (but your teacher will in any case pitch the level of questions at your actual ability within these levels).

After each question on the CD, there will be a short pause as a cue for you to give your own

1 Speaking

REVISION SUMMARY

answer. For most questions, you will need longer, so pause the CD yourself and restart it once you have answered. You will then hear a sample answer by a German speaker.

The questions you will hear on the CD are not printed in the book. You will not have them in front of you in written form on the day of the Oral Examination. You need to get used to the sound of these questions. First, try to answer the questions which you can do without any extra preparation and perfect these by listening to the answers on the CD. Then attempt the others. If some still seem hard to answer well, keep practising, but bear in mind that some are for the A*/A grade candidate!

If you are not aiming at a grade beyond E, your answers can be quite short. If you are aiming higher, the teacher will develop a conversation with you based on a few key questions. You should try to answer each question as fully as possible, but be prepared for the teacher to interrupt you to check on something or to ask another question.

The topics are covered in the following order, first at Foundation level (up to grade E), then at Higher level (beyond grade E):

- Topic A – *Deine Familie* (Foundation) – *Dein Freund* (Higher)
- Topic B – *Haus und Heim*
- Topic C – *Deine Stadt*
- Topic D – *Schule*
- Topic E – *Freizeit und Hobbys*
- Topic F – *Ferien*
- Topic G – *Das Wetter und die Jahreszeiten*
- Topic H – *Zukunftspläne* (Higher only, covering further education and work)

NOTE: At the end of the Role Play Tasks, you will find some Examiner's comments on General Conversation on CD.

These should be read before you attempt to answer the questions yourself!

3 Finally, prepare a Presentation. Whether or not your Board requires you to carry out this task, it would help you to develop your oral skills if you listen carefully to the Presentation and the following discussion on the CD.

If your Board does set this task, it may come after the Role Play and before the General Conversation in your exam. However, it has been placed last on the CD, because it demands more concentration to listen to and more time to study properly.

After the Examiner's comments on the General Conversation later in this section of the book, you will find some comments on the Presentation and some on the Discussion. The best way to proceed would be to listen first to the Presentation, then to read the comments before listening for a second or further time. Follow the same method with the Discussion.

When you have listened a few times in conjunction with the comments, try to prepare your own Presentation on paper and then practise recording it. Finally, think up some questions that your teacher might want to ask and try to answer these.

If you need to revise this subject more thoroughly, see the relevant topics in the Letts GCSE German Study Guide.

Speaking 1

ROLE PLAYS

FOUNDATION

Unless you hear the teacher say on the CD (after introducing the task) *Ich beginne*, you should speak first in each Role Play (Tasks A to H).

Role Plays at Foundation Level will be based on a visual stimulus, in other words you will have to interpret pictures or icons. Your Board may have produced a guide for teachers in order to explain the meaning of the pictures it will use in these tasks. Ask your teacher! The tasks for each Role Play will also be set out in English.

You stop a passer-by and ask the way to the railway station. After the teacher has set the scene, you start the conversation.

TASK A

1   2   3 100m 1km 5km   4   5

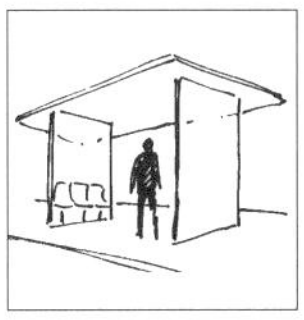

Examiner's tip   Make sure you have seen and understood any booklet of icons/pictures produced by your Board. You do not want to waste valuable preparation time in trying to interpret a picture. You will notice that there is often more than one way of saying things.
2 You could ask either *Wo ist der Bahnhof?* or *Wie komme ich am besten zum Bahnhof?*
3 You could get away with using one of the distances given and ask *Ist es hundert Meter von hier?* Normal question would be *Ist es weit?/Wie weit ist es?* If you can't remember *weit*, ask *Ist es in der Nähe?*
4 *Wo ist der Bus?* is not suitable here. You could use that, if stuck, on 5. You need: *Kann ich mit dem Bus fahren?*

You are talking to a German teenager of the opposite sex at a party. You start the conversation by asking him/her about his/her family.

TASK B

1 Er/Sie?   2 Du?   3 Er/Sie?

4 Er/Sie?   5 Er/Sie?

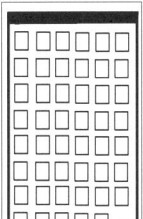

Examiner's tip   **1/2** Remember that *Geschwister* means 'brothers and sisters'.
3 If you can't remember 'pets' (*Haustiere*), you could just ask *Hast du eine Katze (oder einen Hund)?*
4 If you have forgotten the German names for specific types of dwelling (*in einem Einzelhaus/in einer Wohnung*), just ask *Wohnst du in einem Haus oder in einer Wohnung?*

1 Speaking

TASK C

You are at the post office, where you wish to send two letters and a parcel to England and make a phone call.

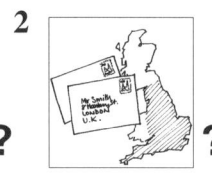

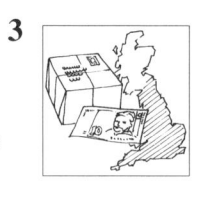

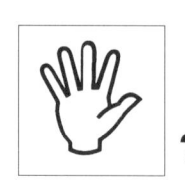

1 2 3 4 5

> **Examiner's tip**
> 2 Simple way of putting it: *Was kosten zwei Briefe nach England?*
> 4 Either *Kann ich telefonieren?* or *Gibt es hier ein Telefon?* or *Wo ist das Telefon?*

FOUNDATION AND HIGHER

Role Plays at this level will be based on a stimulus in German or a visual stimulus, dependent on your Board. Ask your teacher! The tasks for each Role Play will also be set out in English.

In the Foundation and Higher as well as the Higher Role Play, you will always be required to reply to (at least) one question or statement from the examiner (see Task D). Your card will not tell you what this will be about. Whilst preparing, you should spend a little time thinking what this might be and how to answer it.

TASK D

Kandidat(in): auf Urlaub in Deutschland
Lehrer(in): Arzt (Ärztin)

Sie verbringen Ihre Ferien in Deutschland. Nach einigen Tagen fühlen Sie sich nicht wohl. Sie gehen zum Arzt (zur Ärztin).
(You are on holiday in Germany. After a few days there you feel unwell and go to the doctor's.)*

1 Erklären Sie, was Sie in Deutschland machen.
2 Sagen Sie, was mit Ihnen los ist (eine Erkältung).
3 Beantworten Sie die Frage.
4 Sagen Sie welche Symptome Sie haben.
5 Bedanken Sie sich und fragen Sie nach der nächsten Apotheke.

UCLES 1996

* The introduction to the Role Play will usually be in English on your card, but the teacher will normally read a German version to you before the Role Play begins.

> **Examiner's tip**
> 1 You have time to prepare this. You could say *Ich bin auf Urlaub in Deutschland* or *Ich besuche meinen Brieffreund (meine Brieffreundin)*. If you forget what you wanted to say, you can reword the teacher's introduction which he/she will read out to you before you begin: *Ich verbringe meine Ferien in Deutschland*.
> 2 Either *Ich habe eine Erkältung* or *Ich bin erkältet*. You may be given no clues on your card and may have to make up some illness – see 4.
> 3 At this level there will be an unpredictable element. Here you know in advance from your preparation that you must listen very carefully to what the teacher asks, since your card gives you no clue. Your answer will have to start with *seit* (+ dative), e.g. *seit zwei Tagen* or, picking up what the teacher said in the introduction, *seit einigen Tagen*.
> 4 *Symptome* is plural, so you need to mention at least two ailments.

Speaking 1

TASK E

Kandidat(in): in einem Hotel
Lehrer(in): Empfangsperson in einem Hotel

Sie sind seit gestern in einem deutschen Hotel, aber Sie sind mit Ihrem Zimmer unzufrieden. Sie sprechen mit der Empfangsperson.
(You arrived in a German hotel yesterday but are dissatisfied with your room. You speak to the receptionist.)

1 Begrüßen Sie die Empfangsperson und stellen Sie sich vor (Name, Zimmernummer).
2 Sagen Sie, daß Sie mit Ihrem Zimmer unzufrieden sind, und erklären Sie, warum (Nennen Sie zwei Gründe.).
3 Reagieren Sie auf die Antwort der Empfangsperson (Sie wollen in Ihrem Zimmer nicht bleiben. Was sagen Sie?).
4 Beantworten Sie die Fragen nach dem Zimmer und Ihrem Aufenthalt.
5 Reagieren Sie auf die Antwort der Empfangsperson.

UCLES 1995

Examiner's tip
2 You should have prepared two reasons. Can you suggest different possibilities from the ones on CD?
3 It is not enough to re-arrange the statement on the card and say only *Ich möchte nicht in dem Zimmer bleiben*. You need to add that you want another room.
5 The unpredictable element. Threaten to change hotels or to cut your stay short! Don't just give in by accepting to stay in your present room.

TASK F

Kandidat(in): Sie selbst zu Hause – am Telefon
Lehrer(in): deutscher Freund (deutsche Freundin) auf Urlaub in Ihrem Land

Ihr deutscher Freund (Ihre deutsche Freundin) ist auf Urlaub in Ihrem Land und wohnt nicht weit von Ihrem Haus entfernt. Er/sie ruft Sie an.
(Your German friend is on holiday in your country and staying near to where you live. He/she telephones you.)

1 Begrüßen Sie Ihren Freund (Ihre Freundin), und fragen Sie, wo er/sie sich befindet.
2 Sagen Sie, daß Sie sich auf ein Wiedersehen freuen.
3 Sagen Sie, wann Sie frei sind, und schlagen Sie einen Treffpunkt vor.
4 Sagen Sie, was Sie mit Ihrem Freund (Ihrer Freundin) unternehmen könnten (Nennen Sie zwei Ideen.).
5 Reagieren Sie auf die Antwort Ihres Freundes (Ihrer Freundin), und erklären Sie, wie er/sie den Treffpunkt erreichen kann.

UCLES 1995

Examiner's tip
1–4 All these should be well prepared in advance. 1/2 require you to reword the German on the card considerably. 3/4 demand imagination.
5 You need to listen carefully and follow up your friend's choice of activity here, before stating the imaginary directions/travel arrangements which you prepared.

1 Speaking

HIGHER

These tasks will be based on a stimulus in German with the possibility of a visual stimulus, dependent on your Board.

The following task (Task G) is based on a stimulus in German.

TASK G

Candidate's role

You make a telephone call to your German friend to arrange his/her visit to your house during your summer holiday in July or August.

You have made some notes to help you. Be prepared to change your plans to suit your friend. You start the conversation.

> Besuch von Dieter/Inge
>
> August ... zwei Wochen?
>
> schwimmen? andere Aktivitäten?
>
> Ausflüge mit dem Bus?
>
> Sehenswürdigkeiten in der Nähe?

Examiner's tip This task is open-ended. The teacher will ask you a number of questions which are not indicated on your card. You will be expected to discuss and negotiate. When preparing you could expect that your penfriend would prefer a different month, activity and place to visit from those that you are suggesting. So work out some spare suggestions in advance.

NARRATOR TASK

The following task (Task H) is based on a visual stimulus with some guidance in German.

- The notes printed below give an outline of one day of a camping holiday with German friends.

TASK H

- Tell the Examiner about the day. You can decide if it was you or someone else who went camping. You need not mention every detail but you must cover the whole event.

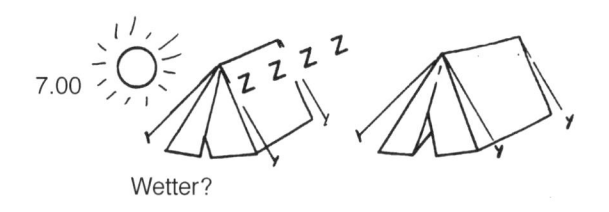

- Be prepared to respond to any questions or observations the Examiner may make.

7.00

Wetter?

Was gemacht? | Toiletten | Waschraum |

7.45   Frühstück

Nach dem Frühstück – was gemacht?

Speaking 1

9.00	Wohin?	SUPERMARKT	Was gekauft?	

10.30	Wohin?	Geschwommen?

12.45	Picknick – Wo? Was gegessen?	Am Nachmittag – was gemacht?

Am Abend – was gemacht?

MEG 1994

Examiner's tip   The indications on the card form an outline for your account of what happened. You should make good use of them. You must use the past tenses, either the simple past *(Ich fuhr nach Deutschland.)* or the perfect *(Ich bin nach Deutschland gefahren.)*.
For this you have to learn your verb tables. If you are using the perfect tense, you should also learn which verbs need *sein* instead of *haben*.
Even if you are using the perfect tense, you still need to revise the imperfect tense of *sein*, *haben* and of the modal verbs *dürfen, können, müssen, sollen, wollen*.
Your narrative will sound better if you can link sentences together, e.g.
without link word: *Ich bin um sieben Uhr aufgestanden. Ich habe mich gewaschen.*
with link word: *Ich bin um sieben Uhr aufgestanden. Dann habe ich mich gewaschen.*
Note: the change in word order (underlined).
You should also try to make up sentences with a subordinate clause (using *weil, als, dass, bis,* etc.) e.g. Task H:
Das Frühstück hat mir nicht geschmeckt, weil das Brot zu alt war NOTE: the word order (underlined).
You will achieve a higher mark if you give your opinions, e.g. say what you thought about the food/the evening/the whole day.
Specimen answer on CD
Listen for examples on the CD which correspond to the tips given above.
Here is some help with vocabulary used in the specimen answers. Only less well-known items of vocabulary are explained in the rest of the Speaking section.
schnarchen = to snore
eine Frikadelle = a rissole/meatball

1 Speaking

GENERAL CONVERSATION

There are two parts: help is given with vocabulary in

1 Teacher's questions
2 Answers

You should read Part **1** before you listen to the questions being read on the recording. You should have Part **2** in front of you as you listen to the specimen answers.

TEACHER'S QUESTIONS

FOUNDATION

TOPIC C – *Deine Stadt*
4 *Sportanlagen* = sports facilities.

TOPIC G – *Das Wetter und die Jahreszeiten*
2 *erwarten* = to expect.

HIGHER

TOPIC C – *Deine Stadt*
2 *unternehmen* = (to) do.
3 *die Umgebung* = (here) the area around your town.

TOPIC F – *Ferien*
1 *feiern* = to celebrate.

TOPIC H – *Zukunftspläne*
2 *Leistungskurse* = (here) your A-level courses.
3 (*einen Beruf*) *ausüben* = to follow (a career).
4 *eine Lehre* = an apprenticeship.
5 *die Aussichten* = (here) the prospects.

ANSWERS

FOUNDATION

TOPIC A – *Deine Familie*
2–3 At Foundation level, your answers do not need to be as long as those on the tape. They are there to give you some ideas.
2 *glatt* = straight (hair).
3 *gelockt* = curly (hair).

TOPIC B – *Haus und Heim*
2 *geräumig* = roomy/large.
4 *der Teich* = pond.

TOPIC C – *Deine Stadt*
4 *Bowling(bahn)* = tenpin bowling; *Kegel(bahn)* = ninepin.

TOPIC E – *Freizeit und Hobbies*
7 *Action* = action (borrowed from English!).

HIGHER

TOPIC B – *Haus und Heim*
3 *Zeitungen austragen* = deliver newspapers.

TOPIC C – *Deine Stadt*
2 *stattfinden* = to take place/to be held.
3 *eine Mine* = a mine.

TOPIC D – *Schule*
1 *sich unterhalten* = to talk/chat.
2 *Musikprobe* = rehearsal.
3 *gestreift* = striped.
Last question: *abschaffen* = do away with/get rid of.

TOPIC E – *Freizeit und Hobbies*
1 *eine Pizzeria* = a pizza hut; *der Abwasch* = washing-up.
3 *der Abenteuerroman* = adventure novel.

TOPIC F – *Ferien*
2 Note the pronunciation of *eine CD* (as you say the letters 'C' and 'D' in German) = a compact disk.
5 *sich (um etwas) kümmern* = to worry (about something).
9 (about the exchange) *aufregend* = exciting.

TOPIC H – *Zukunftspläne*
1 *eine Ausbildungsstelle* = a job as an apprentice.
5 *sich (bei einer Firma/um eine Stelle) bewerben* = to apply (to a firm/for a job).
Last question: *das Kanu* = canoe.

Speaking 1

PRESENTATION

Examiner's comments

You will notice that the candidate's chosen topic covers the areas of food and drink, health and fitness, and the environment. These are GCSE topics which were not included in the General Conversation on the CD. For the topic of the environment, you will need to learn some specific new vocabulary.

- You are able to prepare your Presentation in advance of the examination, so there is no harm in looking up words in the dictionary, in order to make some interesting points.
- However, don't be too ambitious. You need to be able to speak in normal German sentences. Your speech must not sound like a poor translation from English. You also need to understand what you have prepared and be able to answer questions on it. It is best to keep to a topic you know well and which is not too complicated.
- Don't be put off by the A* performance of the candidate on the CD. Try to learn some good German from it.
- The candidate introduces the topic and explains how she became interested in it.
- There is a clear structure and development of points. She deals one by one with: smoking, eating, drinking.
- She shows how her views have changed and what she plans to do as a result together with: her friends, her mother, her father.
- This leads her to the final aspect of the environment, where she shows, as she did with the other aspects, why the topic concerns us all. If you do have a topic which is not completely personal, do explain its importance for other people. This makes it more interesting – for the teacher who is listening and to any examiner(s) from your Examination Board who listen(s) to it later on the cassette.

Vocabulary

bis vor kurzem	= until a short while ago
regelmäßig	= regularly
sich ändern	= to change/alter
auf etwas aufmerksam machen	= to draw somebody's attention to something
grausam	= (here) terrible/awful
weiterfahren (*sie fuhr weiter*)	= to go on/continue (she went on)
schädlich	= harmful
viel Schaden anrichten	= to cause a lot of harm
nahrhaft	= nourishing/nutritious
nötig	= necessary
die Fertigpackung (-en)	= pre-packaged food
die Nahrung (no pl.)	= food
ausgeglichen	= balanced
erwähnen	= to mention
erstaunt	= astonished
sei	= present subjunctive form of *sein*
hin und wieder	= now and again
die Wirkung (-en)	= the effect
statt/anstatt … (zu tun)	= instead (of doing)
begeistert	= enthusiastic
überreden	= to convince
sich Gedanken machen	= to think or worry
die Verpackung (-en)	= the packaging/wrapping
der Müll (no pl.)	= rubbish
tatsächlich	= indeed
verrückt	= crazy
verhungern	= to die of hunger/starve to death

1 Speaking

DISCUSSION

Examiner's comments

- As in the Presentation, there are some other words which may be new to you, but you should be able to work them out from the context.
- Note how the teacher follows up the points made by the candidate in her Presentation, asking for further explanations:
  Why was the doctor's talk arranged?
  Why was the beginning of the talk not interesting?
  What did your friends think of the talk?
  Why did you change your lifestyle?
  What does your mother/your father think about the change?
  What do you think about alcohol?
- The teacher is faced with a good candidate, so he usually lets her answer at some length. However, the teacher does prompt with the questions listed above and occasionally checks on something the candidate says – for example, asking whether the PE teacher's opinion of the class is justified.

  As in the General Conversation, the teacher has to keep a balance in the Discussion between stopping you reciting another speech and interrupting you too often.

  Just how frequently the teacher butts in when you are talking will depend on how much material you have prepared and how well you can develop it further in discussion. If you have said all you know how to say on the topic in your Presentation, then both you and the teacher are in for a rough ride in the Discussion: try to keep something in reserve for the Discussion.

Vocabulary

der Rat (pl. *Ratschläge*)	= advice
meckern	= to moan
wären	= imperfect subjunctive of *sein*
hätten	= imperfect subjunctive of *haben*
die Kraft	= strength
gruselig	= horrifying/gruesome
der Eindruck (¨-e)	= impression
deutlich	= clearly
verschiedene	= various
betonen	= to emphasise
wichtig	= important
deshalb	= therefore
das Fett (-e)	= fat
der Grund (¨-e)	= reason
die Mühe lohnt sich	= it is worth the trouble
einem etwas ansehen	= to see something by looking at somebody
mit etwas einstimmen	= to agree with something
sich (Dativ) *über etwas Sorgen machen*	= to worry about something
der Verstand (no pl.)	= the mind/ability to think
die Tat (-en)	= deed/action
die Not (no pl.)	= distress/need/poverty
die Umwelt	= environment
die Umgebung	= surroundings/environment
wieder verbrauchen	= to re-use

Listening 2

ASSESSMENT OBJECTIVES

The GCSE Listening examination will test your ability to do the following, so practise doing them.

1) Foundation
- Identify main points.
- Extract specific details.

2) Foundation and Higher
In addition to Foundation:
- identify points of view/opinions;
- understand reference to past and future events (as well as present).

3) Higher
- Identify attitudes and emotions.
- Draw conclusions, make inferences, recognise relationships between ideas.

At Higher level, any one stimulus might be used to test more than one of the points listed above. The recording accompanying this book includes examples of all these types of test.

All stimulus material will be of the type which you might hear if you listened to a native speaker of the foreign language either in your own country or in the speaker's country. In other words it is designed to be heard and is natural speech. At Higher level, you may have to cope with natural hesitation, spontaneous rephrasing and some background noise.

QUESTION TYPES

A variety of question types will be set by all Examination Boards in both the Listening and the Reading papers. All the following are possible, but may not, of course, be set every year:
- matching visuals/pictures to a text;
- true/false – perhaps with a 'not mentioned (in text)' column;
- multiple choice (with three or perhaps four possible written answers);
- other box-ticking exercises, e.g. ticking appropriate items in a list;
- completing grids or tables;
- selecting from a list the sentences which match the text;
- sequencing of sentences or pictures in relation to a text;
- gap-filling, note or sentence completion in German or in English*;
- writing answers in English to questions in English*;
- writing answers in German to questions in German.

* Exercises requiring the use of English are limited to 20% of the Listening and Reading papers – Boards may use less than 20%.

NOTE: only two Boards, WJEC and NEAB, allow dictionaries for the Listening paper. They specify that a bilingual dictionary may be used before and after the tape is played, but not whilst the tape is being played. WJEC gives no time indication, but NEAB states five minutes before and after the tape is played.

2 Listening

REVISION SUMMARY

EXAMINATION TECHNIQUE

1) Quality of language produced in answers

Language produced by candidates in answer to a question will not be marked for its quality. The essential requirement is to **communicate** the answer. You will only lose marks if the message you are trying to put across is unclear.

2) Why is listening so difficult in an examination?

When you read a text, you take it at your own speed. The greatest problem which you face in a listening comprehension test is that you are not in control of the text. GCSE examinations do not allow you to stop the tape or to rewind it. (NEAB allows the teacher to stop the tape, but only for the candidates to write their answers at the end of extracts.) For a number of candidates, this loss of control over foreign speech, which always seems to go faster than their own, causes a sense of panic once the examination is under way, and they do not do as well as expected.

Don't panic! Read the question. You are allowed to look at the questions before you hear each extract, and you should make good use of this time to make sure you read them carefully and understand them.

However, on the first hearing, try to understand the dialogue/monologue **as a whole**, while it is being played. Then only afterwards in the pause before the second playback, try to answer specific questions.

Unless you are very confident of your listening ability, it is not wise to aim at answering specific questions on a longer passage as you listen for the first time. In so doing, you could miss details that are important for other questions and start to worry that you have not understood the passage. It is better to gain in confidence by feeling that you have understood all or most of the material the first time round.

If after the first playback you find that your general understanding of the material allows you to answer some questions, then by all means write down these answers in the pause before you listen for a second time.

During the second playback, you should be able to answer all the questions **in your head** before writing them down in the time available at the end of the recording. Make sure your answers are legible and clearly worded. Sentences are not always required, but at Higher level, statements need to be complete as well as precise.

Owing to the fact that candidates are not able to review and scan the text at leisure in a Listening test, they are even more likely to make mistakes than in a Reading test.

COMMON ERRORS

Here is a list of common errors to avoid in Listening and Reading, with positive remedies. You will find specific examples of these in the tips given with the specimen answers.

- **Don't** muddle up the key question words: *Wann? Wo? Wer? Was? Wie?*, etc. See the Speaking chapter for help on question words.
- **Don't** make vague or over-simplified responses. Be precise. Add all required detail.
- **Don't** add material that is irrelevant to the question or which belongs to another question. It will not gain any credit.
- **Don't** hedge your bets. Many candidates lose marks by guessing at a list of possibilities. You should leave only one clear answer on your script. Plump for one. Cross out others! In the case of box-ticking questions, it is also crucial to make sure that the right number of boxes have been ticked.

Listening 2

- **Don't** guess, unless you are really desperate not to leave a blank space. Try to reason out a response which makes sense from what you have heard/read.
- **Don't** single out isolated words and make up an answer based on these. This will work only in some simpler questions at Foundation level. Listen carefully to/read the whole context.
- **Don't** assume that you have heard a particular word just because it sounds rather like a word you know. Concentrate only on the sound you actually hear and work from that.

HOW TO REVISE FOR LISTENING

Before the examination, try to listen to as much extra German as you can outside school hours. Possibilities include:
- the CD accompanying this book
- cassettes available from your teacher
- cassettes of past examinations (but these are expensive)
- a German penfriend or friend of your family
- German radio or television via cable and satellite
- BBC/Independent Television programmes for schools

WHAT TO REVISE FOR LISTENING

1) Word confusion
Note this list of words which are often confused and check their meanings:

kein/klein	*größer/Größe*
Brot/Brat(wurst, etc.*)*	*getrennt/Getränke*
Sahne taken to mean 'sauce'	*Schinken* thought to be 'chicken'
zwei/drei	numbers in *-zehn/-zig*
Kuchen/kochen	*Café/Kaffee*
rechts/direkt	*blau/braun/grau*
März/Mai	*Dienstag/Donnerstag*
Bahnhof/Bauernhof	*Bahn/Straßenbahn*
nur/neu	*Rasen/Rosen*
Gebühr/Geburt	*D-Mark/Dänemark*

2) Note the different meaning caused by a prefix (underlined):
sehen, to see; *ansehen*, to look at; *aussehen*, to appear/seem
gehen, to go; *mitgehen*, to go with; *ausgehen*, to go out
stehen, to stand; *aufstehen*, to stand up/get up; *ausstehen*, to stand in the sense of 'put up with/tolerate'.
Flug, flight; *Abflug*, departure (of plane); *Ausflug*, excursion/trip
Schrift, (hand)writing; *Anschrift*, address; *Unterschrift*, signature

Listen out for the prefix *-un* which makes an opposite as in English. It should be easy to spot it in a Reading text, but it may be missed when you listen to a tape, e.g. *(un)freundlich*, (un)friendly; *(un)glücklich*, (un)happy.

2 Listening

REVISION SUMMARY

3) Partial hearing
Another frequent error is to hear only part of a word:
Nachmittag heard as *Mittag* or *Nacht*, *Handschuhe* taken to be *Handtasche* and vice-versa.

4) Cognates and near-cognates
As you will have noticed in the Speaking unit, a cognate means a word which has the same spelling and meaning in English as in German. But note the difference in sound, e.g. *Ball, blind, blond, England, Gold, Hand, intelligent, Kilometer, Margarine, Minute, modern, Museum, Name, normal, Orange, Patient, Person, Portion, Problem, Religion, Ski, Station, warm, Zoo.*

Near-cognate means a word which has the same meaning in both languages but a slightly different spelling. Again note the different sound, e.g. *Kathedrale, Klinik, Konzert, Medizin, Orchester, Salat, Sandale*.

You may skip over these words as you read them, because the meaning is obvious to you. For the Listening test, however, you need to know **how they sound**. It is surprising how many candidates fail to recognise seemingly simple words when listening to a tape. The fact that these words have to be picked out from many others in sentences makes it more difficult. So train your ear by reading vocabulary out **aloud** when you revise.

For more help with cognates, near-cognates and false cognates, see the introduction to the Reading section.

WHAT TO REVISE FOR LISTENING AND READING

You will need to revise your passive vocabulary (how well you know the English meaning of German words) regularly, preferably on a daily basis. See the Speaking section for advice about vocabulary books.

Of course you should be familiar with your whole syllabus, but some small items take little time yet save many marks.

At Foundation level, **numbers** (on their own, or in prices and times), **time expressions** (including clock time, days of the week, months) and **colours** often occur. These are relatively easily learnt to prevent an unnecessary loss of marks.

At Higher level in particular, negative expressions are often used but are overlooked by candidates. This leads to an answer which is the opposite of the truth. Learn the following:

nicht, not	*nichts*, nothing
nie, never	*niemand*, nobody
nicht mehr, no longer	*kein*, no/none
weder... noch, neither... nor	
nicht nur... sondern auch, not only... but also	

Candidates also often ignore or mistranslate **qualifying words** (*ziemlich, ein bißchen, ein wenig, ganz, sehr, zu, so, etwa, ungefähr, ein paar, einige,* etc.). Allowance may be made for failure to understand these at Foundation level, but at Higher level it could be costly.

Prepositions: these add precision to the answer. Note the difference between:
vor der Kreuzung; an der Kreuzung; nach der Kreuzung
Viertel vor elf; Viertel nach elf
vor der Post; neben der Post

If you need to revise this subject more thoroughly, see the relevant topics in the Letts GCSE German Study Guide.

Listening 2

LISTENING QUESTIONS

Listen to the extracts on the CD and answer the questions in the tasks which follow. You will hear each extract twice. A bleep will sound at the end of the first playback to indicate that you are about to hear the extract for a second time.

Wie kommt man in die Stadt?
Wählen Sie das Bild, das am besten paßt. Dann kreuzen Sie das richtige Kästchen an.

A   B   C

C ✓ — straßen bahn (1)

FOUNDATION

TASK A

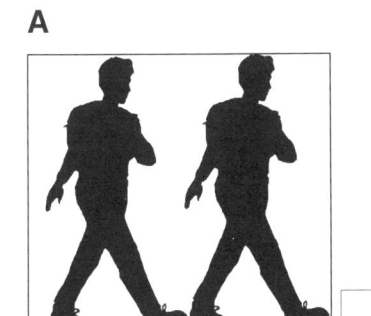

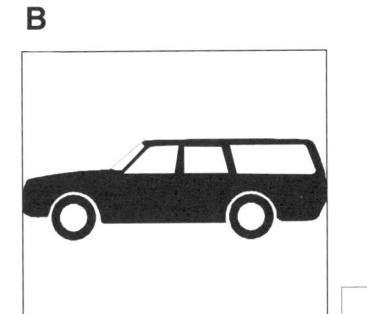

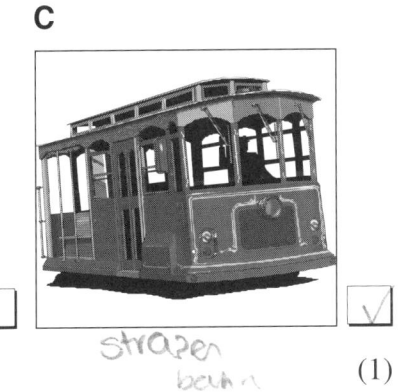

Sie wollen zum Rathaus gehen.

1 Zuerst: Wo biegen Sie ab?

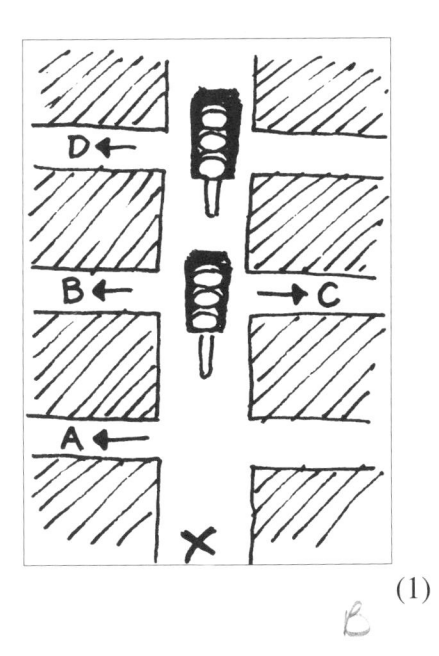

2 Wo liegt das Rathaus?

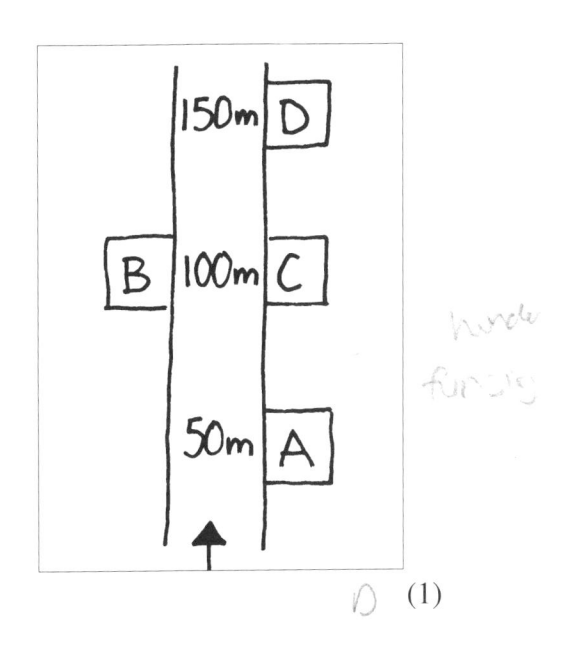

B (1)

D (1)

kinda fürsig

TASK B

21

2 Listening

TASK C

Am Bahnhof
1 Wann fährt der Zug?

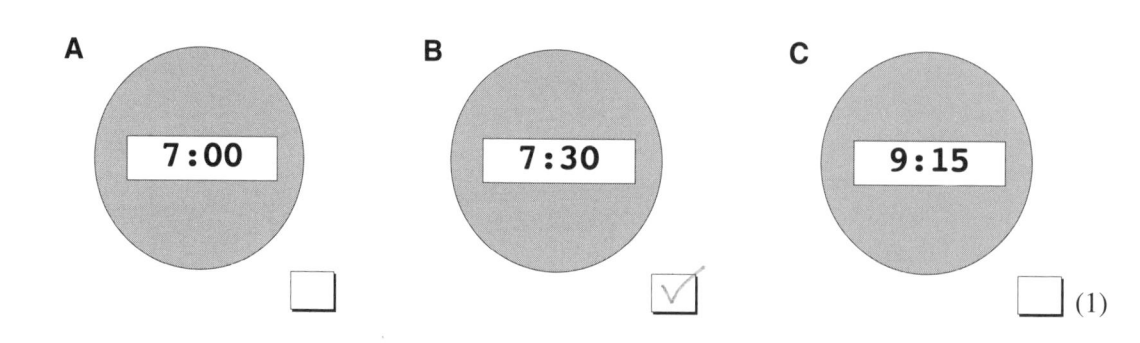

A 7:00 ☐
B 7:30 ☑
C 9:15 ☐ (1)

2 Wo fährt der Zug ab?

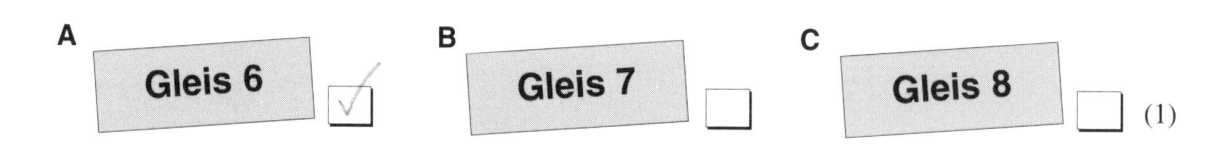

A Gleis 6 ☑
B Gleis 7 ☐
C Gleis 8 ☐ (1)

TASK D

Im Kaufhaus
In welchem Stock finden Sie die folgenden Artikel?
Kreuzen Sie den richtigen Stock an.

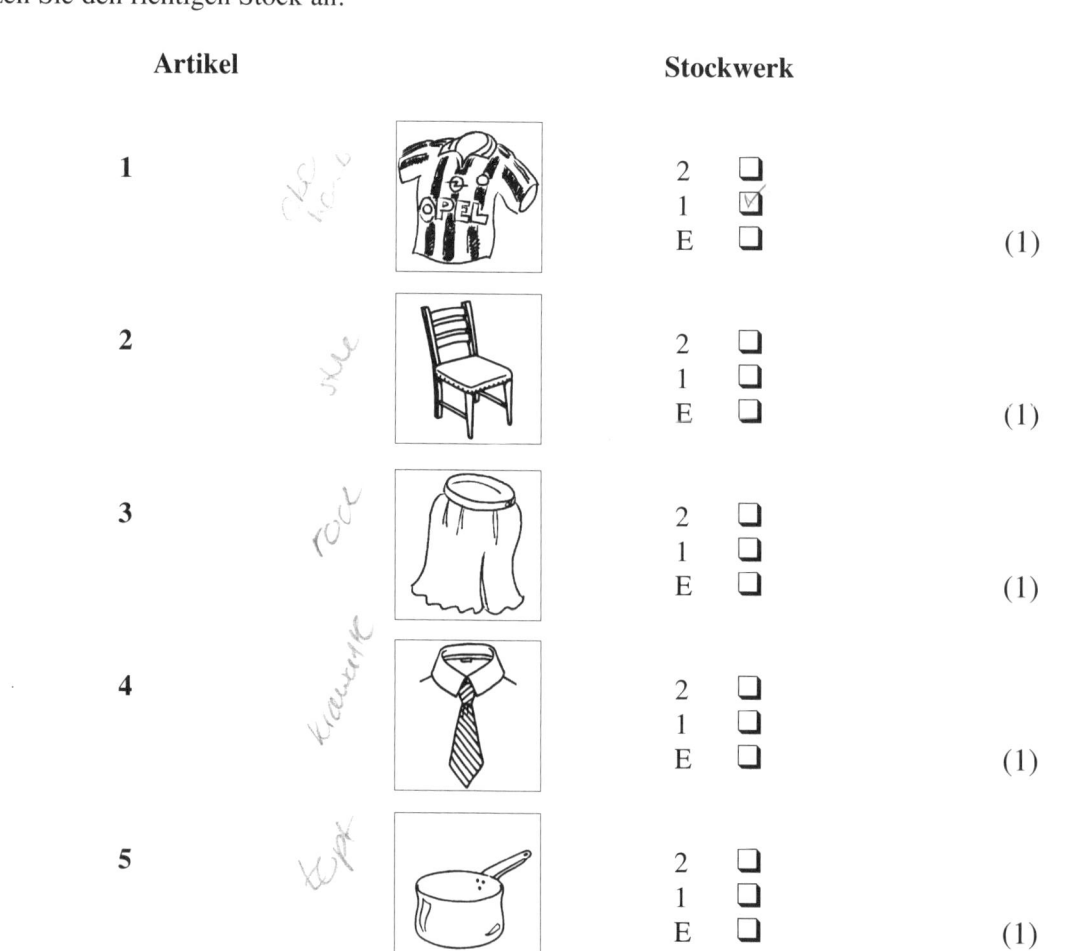

Artikel — Stockwerk

1 2 ☐ 1 ☑ E ☐ (1)

2 2 ☐ 1 ☐ E ☐ (1)

3 2 ☐ 1 ☐ E ☐ (1)

4 2 ☐ 1 ☐ E ☐ (1)

5 2 ☐ 1 ☐ E ☐ (1)

Listening 2

Im Café
Wählen Sie das Bild, das am besten paßt. Dann kreuzen Sie das richtige Kästchen an.

TASK E

TRACK 32

1 Was trinkt Ralf? A [ ]   B [✓]   C [ ] 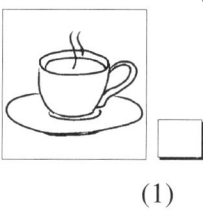
(1)

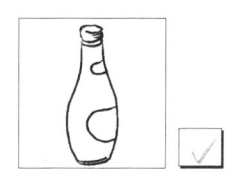

2 Was trinkt Susanne? A [✓]   B [ ]   C [ ] 
(1)

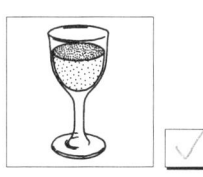

3 Was ißt Susanne? A [✗]   B [✓]   C [ ] 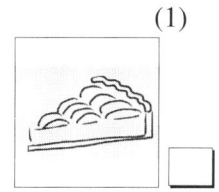
(1)

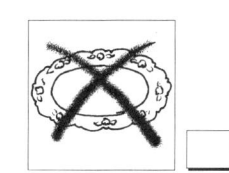

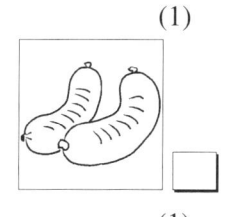

4 Was ißt Ralf? A [✗][✓]   B [ ]   C [ ]
(1)

5 Was kostet alles zusammen?

DM 5,70	A	[ ]
DM 15,70	B	[ ]
DM 7,50	C	[✓]

(1)

23

2 Listening

TASK F

Wilhelms Familie
Füllen Sie die Tabelle auf deutsch aus.
    e.g. NAME   Wilhelm

1 ALTER	15
2 GESCHWISTER	Nein

(1)

(1)

Wählen Sie das Bild, das am besten paßt. Dann kreuzen Sie das richtige Kästchen an.

3 HAUSTIERE

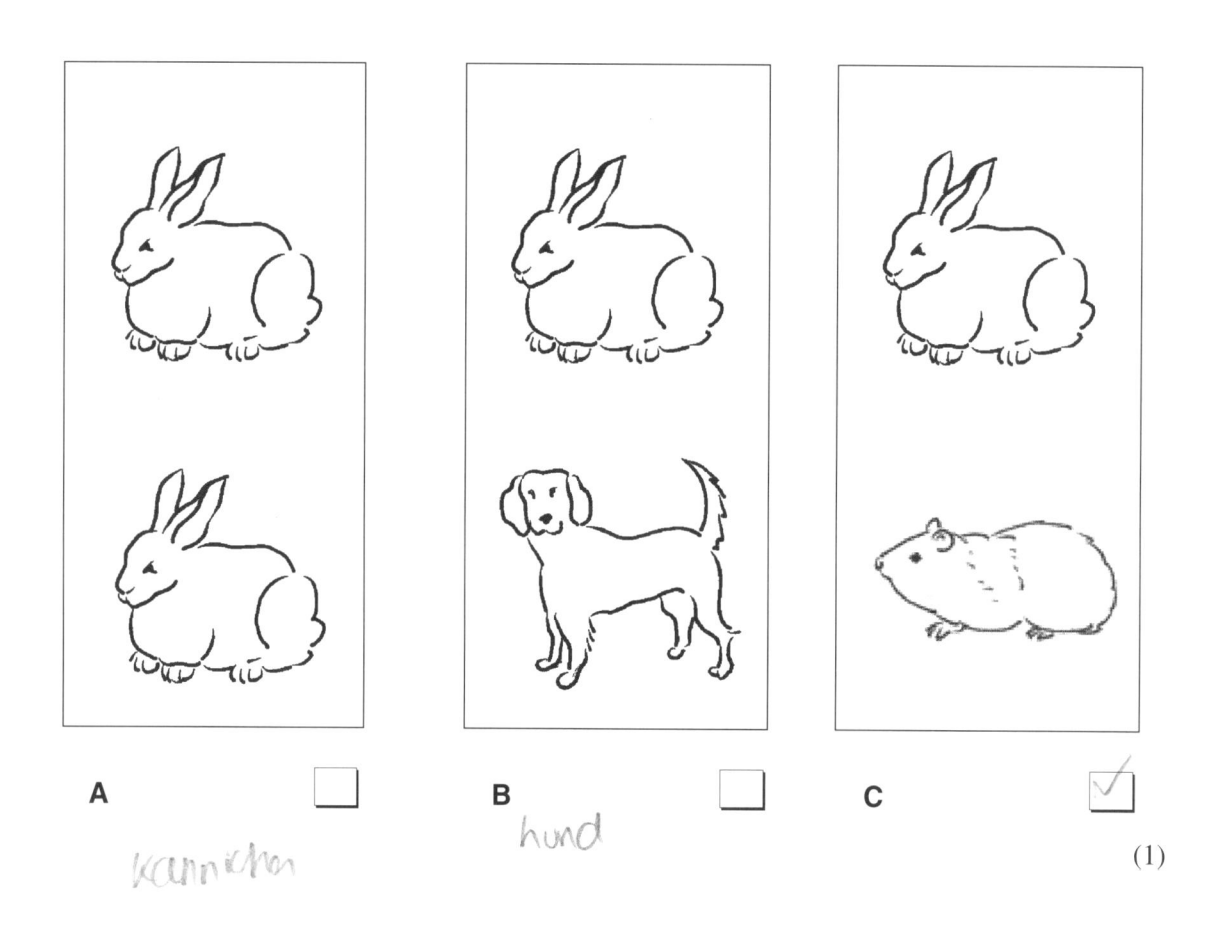

A ☐   B ☐   C ☑

kanninchen   *hund*

(1)

Listening 2

Inges Hobbys
Wählen Sie die Bilder, die am besten passen. Dann kreuzen Sie die richtigen Kästchen an.

FOUNDATION AND HIGHER

TASK G (TRACK 34)

A B C

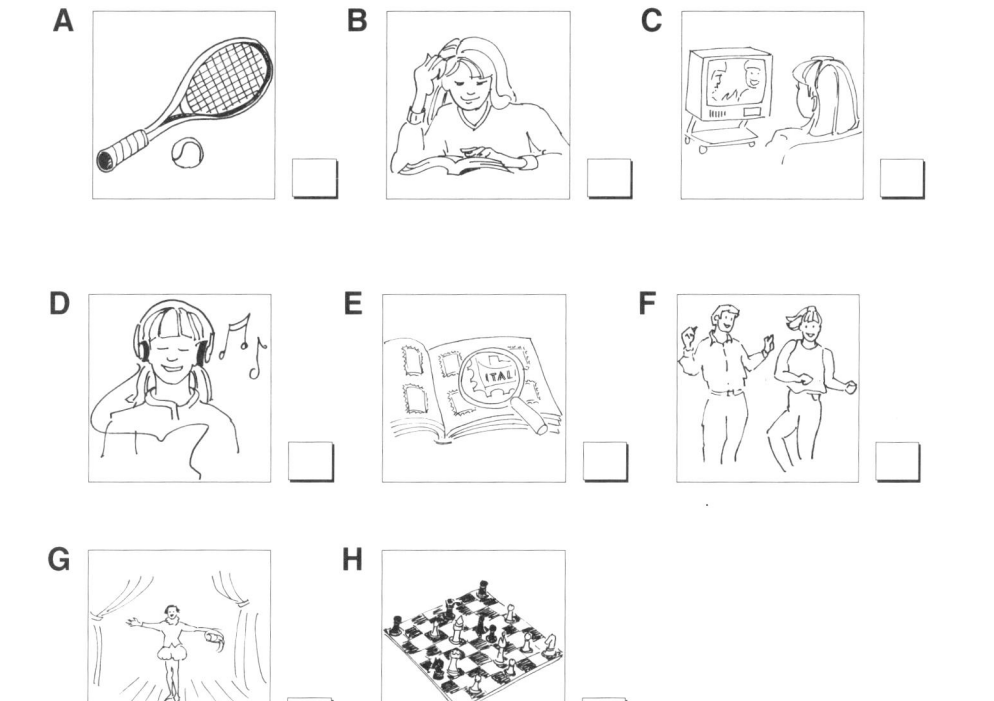

D E F

G H

(4)

In der Schule
Maria und Max sprechen über ihre Schulfächer.
Wählen Sie die Antwort, die am besten paßt, und kreuzen Sie das Kästchen an.

TASK H (TRACK 35, 36)

	NAME	FACH	Wie ist das Fach?					
1	Maria	Geschichte	interessant ☐	langweilig ☐		leicht ☐	(1)
2	Max	Geschichte	nützlich ☐	schwierig ☐		uninteressant ☐	(1)
3	Maria	Mathe	langweilig ☐	lustig ☐		schwierig ☐	(1)
4	Max	Mathe	keine Aussage ☐	leicht ☐		spannend ☐	(1)
		PAUSE					
5	Maria	Englisch	langweilig ☐	leicht ☐		macht Spaß ☐	(1)
6	Max	Englisch	keine Aussage ☐	nützlich ☐		schwierig ☐	(1)
7	Maria	Sport	anstrengend ☐	gut für die Gesundheit ☐		macht Spaß ☐	(1)
8	Max	Sport	anstrengend ☐	gut für die Gesundheit ☐		macht Spaß ☐	(1)
9	Maria	Physik	langweilig ☐	nützlich ☐		schwierig ☐	(1)
10	Max	Physik	keine Aussage ☐	leicht ☐		macht Spaß ☐	(1)

2 Listening

TASK I

Vier Jugendliche sprechen über die Bücher, die sie gerne lesen.
Wer liest gern die folgenden Bücher? Kreuzen Sie die richtige Person an.

Buch	Angelika	Stefan	Brigitte	Kurt	Niemand
1 Liebesgeschichten					
2 historische Geschichten					
3 Detektivgeschichten					
4 Abenteuergeschichten					
5 Naturbücher					
6 Sportbücher					

(6)

TASK J

Jetzt hören Sie zweimal einen Ausschnitt, in dem Arno, ein deutscher Schüler, über seine Berufspläne spricht.

Hören Sie gut zu, und beantworten Sie die Fragen. Wenn die Aussage richtig ist, kreuzen Sie das Kästchen **JA** an. Wenn die Aussage falsch ist, kreuzen Sie das Kästchen **NEIN** an.

Bevor Sie den Ausschnitt hören, lesen Sie bitte die Fragen durch.

		JA	NEIN	
1	Arno hat noch ein Jahr auf der Schule.	☐	☐	(1)
2	Seine Eltern lassen ihn in Ruhe seinen Beruf wählen.	☐	☐	(1)
3	Es ist ihm egal, daß er noch keine festen Pläne hat.	☐	☐	(1)
4	Viele seiner Freunde haben schon einen Beruf gewählt.	☐	☐	(1)
5	Arno sucht schon einen Platz an einer Universität.	☐	☐	(1)
6	Er interessiert sich für Musik.	☐	☐	(1)
7	Er denkt zuletzt an eine Karriere in einer Bank.	☐	☐	(1)
8	Er möchte viel Geld verdienen.	☐	☐	(1)

UCLES 1996

Listening 2

You are listening to your penfriend's elder brother, Werner, talking to a family friend, Frau Müller, about the time he spent in England.

HIGHER
TASK K

(a) What does Werner say about his driving in England? Mention TWO points.

....

.... (2)

(b) What specific problem did he have when he returned to Germany?

.... (1)

(c) What TWO things does Werner say in favour of English public transport?

.... (1)

.... (1)

MEG 1993

Jetzt hören Sie zweimal einen Ausschnitt, in dem Frau Buchholz einem Reporter über den Einbruch in ihr Haus erzählt.

TASK L

Hören Sie gut zu, und ergänzen Sie die Notizen auf deutsch.

Bevor Sie den Ausschnitt hören, lesen Sie bitte die Fragen durch.

Einbruch bei Frau Buchholz

1 Wann genau passierte der Einbruch?

.... (1)

2 Wie ist der Einbrecher ins Haus gekommen?

.... (2)

3 Wie sah der Einbrecher aus?   Alter: .... (1)

                                 Kleidung: .... (1)

4 Wie reagierte der Einbrecher, als er in der Küche gefunden wurde?

.... (2)

5 Wann kam die Polizei an? .... (1)

6 Was ist mit dem Einbrecher passiert?

.... (1)

UCLES 1996

2 Listening

TASK M

Hermann, a friend of your parents who lives in the Rhineland, is talking about *Karneval*, which takes place every year in February.
You will hear what he has to say in two parts.

Part 1

(a) On what day of the week was the carnival procession held?

.... (1)

(b) Apart from giving her balloons, how exactly did Hermann get Ingeborg ready to go out?

.... (1)

(c) What was Ingeborg's attitude to these preparations?

.... (1)

(d) Who else was going to the town?

.... (1)

Part 2

(e) What change has been made in the town since Ingeborg's visit?

.... (1)

(f) What caused Ingeborg's surprise?

.... (1)

(g) What was Hermann's comment about the nature of the carnival?

.... (1)

(h) What is Hermann's overall view of the carnival?

  A He is enthusiastic about it.

  B He is astonished by it.

  C He would rather watch it on TV.

  D It is too crowded.

Write the correct letter here .... (1)

MEG 1994

Reading 3

ASSESSMENT OBJECTIVES

REVISION SUMMARY

The GCSE Reading examination will test your ability to do the following, so practise doing them.

1) Foundation
- Identify main points.
- Extract specific details.

2) Foundation and Higher
In addition to Foundation:
- identify points of view/opinions;
- understand reference to past and future events (as well as present);
- show some understanding of unfamiliar language.

3) Higher
In addition to Foundation/Foundation and Higher:
- identify attitudes and emotions;
- draw conclusions, make inferences, recognise relationships between ideas;
- understand a wider range of language registers.

At Higher level, any one stimulus might be used to test more than one of the points listed above.

STIMULUS MATERIAL AND QUESTION TYPES

This may include the following:
- instructions, signs, notices, menus, timetables, advertisements.
- information leaflets, brochures and guides.
- letters, magazine and newspaper articles.
- imaginative writing – including extracts from books.

For question types, see this heading in the Listening section. The question types listed there also apply to Reading.

NOTE: all Boards allow the use of a dictionary for the Reading paper. MEG allows either a monolingual or a bilingual dictionary, whereas all other Boards specify a bilingual dictionary.

EXAMINATION TECHNIQUE

1) Quality of language used in answers
Language produced by candidates in answer to a question will not be marked for its quality. The essential requirement is to **communicate** the answer. You will only lose marks if the message you are trying to put across is unclear.

2) Common errors
The list of common errors to avoid in the Listening section applies also to Reading. Check these hints first!

3 Reading

REVISION SUMMARY

Don't rush through the papers. You may think some questions are easy, but **do** take great care to get them right. However, don't spend too long on any item which you find difficult. Make a note that you have left it out and come back to it later.

For shorter texts, there is often no need to read and digest every word of print. First look at the questions to find out what you need to know, then scan the text to obtain the answers.

When you are faced with a longer stimulus in continuous writing, with multiple choice answers or answers to be written in English or German sentences, read the text once **before** paying any attention to the questions. This will ensure that you have grasped the overall argument or development of points.

If you are formulating your own answers in English or German, you should then look at **all** the questions before dealing with each question one by one. In this way, you will be offering only the material appropriate to each answer without repetition or needless additional details which belong elsewhere.

As you answer the questions, study each relevant sentence of the text carefully to understand its structure and full meaning. Try to comprehend the whole context. **Don't** pick out isolated words which you can grasp at first glance. Candidates often fail by making this gross error.

Make sure your answers are legible and clearly worded. Sentences are not always required, but statements need to be complete as well as precise, and this can be demanding at Higher level.

Always allow time to **check** your work. When doing so, do make sure that you have not missed any answers. In particular, see if there are any blank pages, by following the page numbers on the papers right up to the last (back) page. Each year, even good candidates lose marks by skipping whole pages.

WHAT TO REVISE FOR READING

1) Sentence structure

In order to understand texts, particularly above Foundation level, you must be very familiar with German syntax or sentence structure. Many candidates make the mistake of revising this only before the Writing paper. It is vital to revise word order for Reading in order to understand the development of points or ideas in a text, instead of lifting out isolated words. Your revision should include the following aspects which would then help you for the Writing paper as well:

- The verb in a simple sentence (main clause only) comes in second position:
  e.g. *Ich fahre nach London.* OR: *Morgen fahre ich nach London.*

- In questions starting with a question word, the main verb also comes second:
  e.g. *Wann bist du angekommen?*

- However, in questions without a question word, the verb comes first:
  e.g. *Gehst du heute abend ins Kino?*

- Past participles and infinitives come at the end of the main clause:
  e.g. *Ich bin nach Cardiff gefahren.*
  Ich muss zur Schule gehen.

- If two main clauses are joined by a co-ordinating conjunction *(aber, denn, oder, sondern, und)*, this is not taken into account when deciding where to put the verb:
  e.g. *Ich bin müde, aber ich bin nicht krank.*
  You can see that this is like English word order.

- In a subordinate clause the verb (or auxiliary) is put at the end. The following are conjunctions which cause the verb to go at the end:
  als = when/as/than   *als ob* = as if

Reading 3

REVISION SUMMARY

bevor/ehe = before   *bis* = until
da = as/since   *damit* = so that
dass = that   *nachdem* = after
ob = whether   *obgleich/obwohl* = although
seit/seitdem = since   *sobald* = as soon as
solange = as long as   *während/indem* = while
weil = because   *wann* = when
wenn = when/if

e.g. *Als ich in York war, habe ich den Dom besichtigt.*
Weil ich das Museum schon besucht hatte*, wollte ich einkaufen gehen.
* NOTE: auxiliary comes last.

- The last two examples also show that after a subordinate clause, the verb in the following main clause (like *habe* or *wollte* above) comes first, that is before the subject *(ich)*.

- The relative pronouns *der/die/das/die* (plural) = who/which and *was* = which also send the verb to the end of the clause:
  Alles, was ich gesehen <u>habe</u>*, hat mir gefallen.*

- In a clause where *zu* is needed with the verb, the infinitive comes at the end:
  e.g. *Ich fahre nach Belfast, um meine Tante zu* <u>besuchen</u>.
  See also **What to revise for Listening** and **What to revise for Listening and Reading** in the Listening section, including cognates.

2) Near-cognates
Many English words resemble German ones. By changing a letter or letters in a German word, you can create an English one or something very close to it. Some examples:

German letter	English letter	German word	English word
b	f	*Dieb*	thief (see -th below)
b	v	*Fieber*	fever
ch	k	*Buch*	book
cht	ght	*Sicht*	sight
d	th	*Ding*	thing
pf	p	*Pfad*	path (see -th above)
t	d	*tanzen*	dance
v	f	*Vater*	father
z	t	*zahm*	tame

You might also note that a number of verbs beginning with *ver-* in German start with 'for-' in English, e.g.: *verbieten* = forbid; *vergeben* = forgive; *vergessen* = to forget.

3) Cognates and near-cognates in sound
These are easy to catch in Listening, but their spelling differs between English and German. Unless you are aware of the sound of the word while you are reading it, you could overlook them in a Reading paper. You may think that *Haus/bevor/Schuh* are obvious, but what about *sauer/Schauer*?

4) False cognates
These are German words which look like English ones but in fact mean something completely different, e.g.: *Chips* = 'crisps'; *fast* = 'almost'; *Kind* = 'child'; *Mappe* = 'briefcase/folder'; *Regal* = 'shelves'.

If you need to revise this subject more thoroughly, see the relevant topics in the *Letts* GCSE *German Study Guide*.

3 Reading

FOUNDATION TASK A

Sie machen einen Schulaustausch in Deutschland und verbringen morgen auf der Schule. Sie wollen einen deutschen Freund in der Schule treffen.

Lesen Sie zuerst seinen Stundenplan für morgen.

08.00	Versammlung:	Begrüßung der Austauschschüler
08.50	Französisch:	Hörübungen - das macht Spaß!
09.40	Mathematik:	Vorbereitung für die nächste Klassenarbeit
10.30	Pause:	draußen auf dem Schulhof
11.00	Freie Stunde:	Bücher zurückgeben, neue ausleihen
12.00	Mittagspause:	Hoffentlich gibt es heute Gulasch!
13.00	Sport:	Heute ist Handball - da kannst du mitmachen. Vergiß deine Sachen nicht!

Wo und wann können Sie Ihren Freund treffen? Schreiben Sie zu jedem Ort die passende Uhrzeit.

1 Kantine   *12.00* (1)

2 Bibliothek   *08.50* (1)

3 Klassenzimmer *09.40* (1)

4 Sprachlabor   .... (1)

5 Turnhalle   *08.00* (1)

6 Aula   .... (1)

UCLES 1996

Reading 3

Sie lesen die Fernsehsendungen für Samstag.
Finden Sie für jede Person eine Sendung. Dann schreiben Sie den Buchstaben der Sendung in das Kästchen.

TASK B

Teil A

A	05.30	Guten Morgen – Morgenmagazin
B	06.30	Kinderprogramm – für Kinder unter sechs Jahren
C	08.00	Cartoons – Asterix, Tom und Jerry
D	09.30	Jugendserie – was für Probleme Teenagers haben
E	10.30	Gesundheitstips – wie man fit bleibt
F	11.00	Allein unter Computern – die neue Technologie
G	12.00	Gott und die Welt
H	13.00	Reiselust – nachts in Paris; die Türkei – Land und Leute
I	14.00	Aktuell – Nachrichten

Welche Sendung paßt zu diesen Personen? Vorsicht! Jeden Buchstaben können Sie nur einmal benutzen.

Beispiel: Maria interessiert sich für Religion.
Antwort: G

1   Max sucht einen Zeichentrickfilm. ☐ (1)

2   Inge will nicht krank werden. ☐ (1)

3   Barbara sieht gern fern, wenn sie frühstückt. ☐ (1)

4   Karl interessiert sich für Informatik. ☐ (1)

5   Lisa sucht etwas für die Kleinen. ☐ (1)

6   Peter will auf Urlaub gehen aber weiß nicht wohin. ☐ (1)

7   Stefanie sucht ein Programm für Jugendliche. ☐ (1)

Teil B

J	14.30	Konzert – Wiener Stadtorchester
K	16.30	Hercules – US-Fantasyserie
L	17.30	Tiersendung – Wir und wildelebende Tiere: Bericht aus Afrika
M	18.45	Marienhof – Familienserie
N	19.40	Wetterbericht
O	19.50	Lottozahlen – sechs Richtige: 2 Millionen Mark
P	20.00	Heute-Journal
Q	20.20	Spielfilm – Komödie
R	22.00	Das aktuelle Sportstudio – alle Sportarten

8   Karoline hat Löwen und Elefanten gern. ☐ (1)

9   Sebastian fragt: "Wird es morgen schön sein?" ☐ (1)

10 Kerstin ist traurig und will über etwas lachen. ☐ (1)

11 Mathias interessiert sich für Musik. ☐ (1)

12 Willy sieht gern Fußballspiele. ☐ (1)

13 Claudia will viel Geld gewinnen. ☐ (1)

3 Reading

TASK C Lies die Texte.

Brieffreunde gesucht

Bin 14 Jahre alt: suche Brieffreund(in). Meine Hobbys: Lesen, Blockflöte, Malen, Musik. Ich habe ein Kaninchen und einen Goldfisch. Schreibe an: **Jochen Hertel**, Wasserturm 9, 62008 Wiesbaden.

Ich, 14, suche Brieffreunde im Alter von 14–16 J. Meine Hobbys: Fußball, Tennis, Tischtennis, Judo. Ich habe einen Hund und einen Hamster. Schreibt bitte mit Bild. Schreibt an: **Nina Köbler**, Am Sonnenberg 4, 20075 Hamburg.

Hey! Wer möchte mich als Brieffreundin? Ich bin 13 Jahre alt. Hobbys: Schlittschuhlaufen, Radfahren, Skifahren, Kino. Ihr solltet 13-15 J. sein. Ich habe eine Katze. Schreibe an: **Yvonne Orthen**, Oststr. 46, 28033 Weyhe.

Wer hat Lust, mir zu schreiben? Ich bin 15 und suche Brieffreunde (innen) nicht älter als 17. Meine Hobbys: Schwimmen, Reiten, Briefmarken, Computer. Ich habe keine Tiere, aber ich möchte eins. Schreibe an: **Thomas Lamatsch**, Finkenweg 2, 80113 Grasbrunn.

1 Welches Bild paßt zu welchem Namen?
   Schreibe die Vornamen in die vier richtigen Kästchen.
   Achtung! Zwei Kästchen bleiben natürlich leer.

(a)    (b)    (c)

(d)    (e)    (f)

(4)

Reading 3

2 Wer sagt das? **Schreibe die Vornamen in die vier richtigen Kästchen. Achtung! Zwei Kästchen bleiben natürlich leer.**

(a) Ich mag Haustiere nicht. ....

(b) Ich möchte ein Foto von dir. ....

(c) Ich finde Bücher, besonders Krimis, ganz toll. ....

(d) Ich möchte gern mein eigenes Pferd. ....

(e) Ich möchte gern einen Brieffreund im Ausland. ....

(f) Ich sehe gern Filme, aber nicht zu Hause mit meinen Eltern. .... (4)

SEG 1997

TASK D

Die Waschmaschine

Wir haben zwei Jungen im Alter von 4 und 5 Jahren und ein Mädchen (7 Jahre). Nur der Elektroherd ist bei uns neu. Unser Kühlschrank ist sehr alt, und den Wagen haben wir verkauft. Seit einem Jahr haben wir auch keinen Fernseher mehr. Und jetzt ist die Waschmaschine kaputt.
Mein Mann hat das Ding schon oft repariert – das hat ihm keinen Spaß gemacht. Ich sagte zu ihm: „Du kannst sie sicher wieder reparieren. Wir haben soviel Wäsche." „Tut mir leid! Das kann ich nicht", kam seine Antwort. Ich will eine neue Waschmaschine kaufen, aber mein Mann braucht das Geld für sein Hobby – er sammelt Modellautos.
„Du kannst doch die Wäsche mit der Hand waschen", meinte er.
„Wenn du mir keine neue Maschine kaufen willst, dann kannst du die Wäsche selber waschen!" antwortete ich.
„Na gut, das tu' ich", sagte er.

Kreuzen Sie das richtige Kästchen an!

1 Wie viele Kinder gibt es in der Familie?

A ☐ 2   B ☐ 3   C ☐ 5   D ☐ 7   (1)

2 Was hat die Familie noch? Kreuzen Sie zwei Kästchen an!

A   B   C   D   E

☐   ☐   ☐   ☐   ☐   (2)

3 Reading

3 Was macht der Mann gern in seiner Freizeit?

A B  C

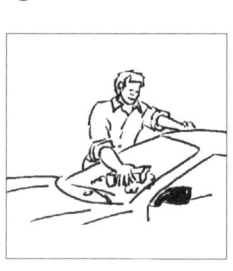

(1)

4 Wer wäscht jetzt die Wäsche, und wie?

A B

C  D

(1)

Reading 3

FOUNDATION AND HIGHER

TASK E

Ein Brief von Sabine aus Dortmund.

> Dortmund, den 1. Mai
>
> Hallo Kathy!
> Ich habe mich sehr über Deinen Brief gefreut. Vielen Dank für die Fotos von Dir und Deiner Familie im Urlaub letzten Monat. Das Wetter zu Ostern war hier nicht so toll wie bei Euch - meist bewölkt und kühl.
> Ich komme bald in die Oberstufe, aber ich weiß noch nicht ganz, was ich für einen Beruf später machen soll. Vielleicht mache ich etwas mit Computern, aber ich bin in Mathe ziemlich schlecht. Meine Eltern finden Computer nicht gut. Sie meinen, daß es zu viele junge Leute gibt, die den ganzen Tag nur am Computer „spielen"!
> Mein Freund Jürgen ist an der Berufsschule. Als Hauptfächer macht er Kochen und Hotelwesen und dazu lernt er Englisch und Mathe. Im kommenden Jahr soll er mit Französisch anfangen. Er ist nicht sehr glücklich darüber – er findet Fremdsprachen schwer. Aber als Koch wird er ein bißchen Französisch brauchen, das weiß er ja.
> Also, das wär's für heute.
> Viele Grüße – auch an Deine Eltern
> Tschüß
>
> Sabine

Wählen Sie die Antwort aus, die am besten paßt. Füllen Sie die Lücken aus!

BEISPIEL:
> Kathy ist Sabines ....
>
> (*Tante*, *Brieffreundin*, *Nachbarin*)
>
> *Antwort*: Kathy ist Sabines *Brieffreundin*.

1 Kathy war .... im Urlaub.
   (*zu Weihnachten*, *zu Ostern*, *im Sommer*) (1)

2 Sabine ...., was sie später als Beruf machen will.
   (*weiß*, *ist nicht ganz sicher*, *hat keine Ahnung*) (1)

3 Sabine ....
   (*ist nicht so gut in Mathe*, *ist sehr gut in Mathe*, *findet Mathe leicht*) (1)

4 Sabines Eltern .... Computer.
   (*sind gegen*, *interessieren sich sehr für*, *spielen den ganzen Tag am*) (1)

5 Jürgen möchte gern ....
   (*Fremdsprachen lernen*, *als Koch arbeiten*, *in Frankreich wohnen*) (1)

MEG 1997

3 Reading

TASK F

„Misses Germany" Simone Aust

Seit der Trennung von ihrem Ehemann lebt Simone Aust mit ihren Kindern in einer Mietwohnung. „Wir haben ein tolles Essen gemacht – Bananen mit Ketchup!" freut sich Susan, die kleine Tochter. Neben Susan am Küchentisch sitzt Christoph, ihr Bruder. Simone lacht und fragt dann: „Und wer macht jetzt sauber?"

Die hübsche Sekretärin hat am 8. Juni die Wahl zur „Misses Germany" gewonnen. Seither darf sich Simone „schönste Ehefrau Deutschlands" nennen. Um diesen Titel zu bekommen, muß man zuerst heiraten!

Doch zu Hause ist die Schönheitskönigin kein Star, sondern ganz liebevolle Mutter, die mit ihren Kindern musiziert, malt oder reiten geht.

„Mein Leben hat sich nach meinem Sieg total verändert", behauptet „Misses Germany". „Ich habe dieses Jahr vor, quer durch Deutschland zu reisen. Ich werde als Modell tätig und in Fernseh- und Radiosendungen zu Gast sein. Sogar der Bundespräsident will mich einladen! Ich freue mich schon darauf."

Füllen Sie die Tabelle auf deutsch aus.
Beispiel: Name: Simone Aust

1	Familienstand:	(1)
2	Kinder (Zahl): (a) Mädchen (b) Jungen	(1)
3	Beruf:	(1)
4	(a) Was gewonnen?	(1)
	(b) Dieser Titel bedeutet:	(1)
5	Freizeitinteressen: (a)	
	(b)	
	(c)	(3)
6	Zukunftspläne: (a)	
	(b)	
	(c)	(3)

Reading 3

Lesen Sie den folgenden Artikel, und beantworten Sie dann die Fragen.

TASK G

Wenn die Aussage richtig ist, kreuzen Sie das Kästchen **JA** an. Wenn die Aussage falsch ist, kreuzen Sie das Kästchen **NEIN** an.

Die Leiden des jungen Jochens

Jeden Morgen, wenn mein Sohn Jochen aufwachte, war er schlecht gelaunt. Er hielt sich dann für schwerkrank.

„Ich habe furchtbare Magenschmerzen", rief er. „Ich glaube, ich werde bald sterben. Niemand interessiert sich dafür. Kein Wunder, daß ich unglücklich bin. Niemand versteht mich."

„Aber wie sollen wir dich denn verstehen?", fragte ich ihn.

„Ach ja, ihr seid genau wie meine Freunde. Mit wem kann man schon reden? Ich muß bloß hier liegen und leiden. Ihr bleibt alle stumm."

Eine Stunde lang beklagte er sich so. Dann sah er, daß es keinen Zweck hatte, da ihm niemand zuhörte. Das war alles nur Theater. Gegen elf Uhr stand er auf. Erst um Mittag wollte er arbeiten.

„Ich weiß nicht, wo ich da anfangen soll", sagte er mir jeden Tag.

Ich wußte nie, was ich antworten sollte. Letzten Samstag fehlten mir aber die Worte nicht mehr.

„In zwei Tagen hast du doch die erste Prüfung. Und du fängst mit Geschichte an, nicht?"

„Ach was! Das ist ganz ohne Interesse."

„Besser ist dann, etwas anderes zu machen, Jochen."

„Aber natürlich, Mutti."

		JA	NEIN	
1	Jochen war wirklich krank.	☐	☐	(1)
2	Seine Eltern konnten ihn nicht verstehen.	☐	☐	(1)
3	Er redete nicht gern mit seinen Freunden.	☐	☐	(1)
4	Er weinte eine Stunde lang vor Schmerzen.	☐	☐	(1)
5	Er fand es schwierig, mit der Arbeit zu beginnen.	☐	☐	(1)
6	Zuerst wollte er Geschichte wiederholen.	☐	☐	(1)

UCLES 1995

3 Reading

TASK H   Lies den Text: aus einer Jugendzeitschrift!

Detlev erzählt von seinem neuen Leben.

Vor einem Jahr hat mein Vater einen neuen Arbeitsplatz in Dresden bekommen. Zunächst mußte er jeden Tag von unserem Wohnort, Kleindorf, vier Stunden mit dem Auto fahren. Das war für ihn sehr anstrengend und es hat auch viel Geld gekostet. Benzin ist ja teuer!

Nach sechs Monaten haben wir eine Wohnung in der Stadtmitte gefunden. Wir wohnen jetzt schon seit vier Monaten hier. Mein Bruder Dirk und ich besuchen jetzt ein Gymnasium in Dresden.

In Kleindorf war wirklich nichts los. Das Stadtleben ist ganz anders. Das Tempo des Verkehrs ist viel schneller. Es gibt aber eine schöne Fußgängerzone. Da gibt's allerlei Geschäfte und ein paar tolle Cafés. Ich fahre auch gern mit der Straßenbahn: das ist wieder was Neues für uns.

Letzte Woche hat sich Dirk das Bein gebrochen. Er ist nämlich vom Fahrrad gefallen. Nächste Woche fahren wir nach Kleindorf, um unsere Großeltern zu besuchen.

Ich vermisse meine Freunde in Kleindorf, aber ich habe schon einige nette Leute in meiner Klasse kennengelernt.

Das Leben hier ist anders, aber es gefällt uns gut.

TEIL A
Ordne die Sätze in der richtigen Reihenfolge. Schreibe 1, 2, 3, 4 oder 5! (5)

(a) Die Jungen haben in einer neuen Schule angefangen. ☐

(b) Der Vater hat einen neuen Job. ☐

(c) Die Familie fährt zu ihren Verwandten. ☐

(d) Die Familie ist umgezogen. ☐

(e) Sein Bruder hat einen Unfall gehabt. ☐

TEIL B
Was findet Dirk _positiv_? Kreuze _ein_ Kästchen an! (1)

(a) Die Autofahrt von Kleindorf nach Dresden. ☐

(b) Den Preis des Benzins. ☐

(c) Freizeit in Kleindorf. ☐

(d) Die Fußgängerzone in Dresden. ☐

(e) Er sieht nur selten seine Freunde in Kleindorf. ☐

WJEC 1998

Reading 3

HIGHER

TASK I

Ein Unfall

Der 10jährige Michael wohnt in einem Hochhaus nicht weit von der Stadtmitte entfernt. Dort hat seine Familie eine Wohnung im fünften Stock.

Michael hat etwas getan, was Jungen so sehr mögen, aber nicht dürfen. Jedesmal, wenn er die Treppen hinunterging, rutschte er auf dem Treppengeländer. Letzte Woche passierte ein Unfall. Der Junge fiel kopfüber 15 Meter in die Tiefe.

Als ihn ein Nachbar einige Minuten später auf dem Boden im Erdgeschoß fand, sah Michael tot aus. Er hatte überall am Körper blaue Flecken und eine Wunde am Kopf. Der Nachbar holte sofort einen Krankenwagen.

Als die Eltern ankamen, war der Junge schon im Krankenwagen.

Michaels Vater sagte zum Polizisten: „Ich hab's schon immer gesagt, er soll das sein lassen. Das Rutschen auf dem Geländer hab' ich ihm verboten."

Die Mutter sagte nur: „Jetzt ist's passiert. Es mußte ja mal so kommen. Tot! Der Junge ist tot!"

Aber der Junge hat es überlebt. Warum hatte er solches Glück? Er fiel auf einen Kinderwagen.

Kreuzen Sie an, ob die Sätze falsch oder richtig sind, oder ob keine Aussage gemacht wird.

		FALSCH	RICHTIG	KEINE AUSSAGE	
1	Michaels Familie hat eine Wohnung in der Stadtmitte.				(1)
2	Michael putzte gern das Treppengeländer.				(1)
3	Ein Nachbar hat den Unfall gesehen.				(1)
4	Als man ihn fand, schien Michael schon tot zu sein.				(1)
5	Der Nachbar rief den Rettungsdienst an.				(1)
6	Die Polizei sagte: "Der Vater ist am Unfall schuld."				(1)
7	Michael durfte nicht auf dem Treppengeländer rutschen.				(1)
8	Der Junge ist im Krankenhaus gestorben.				(1)

3 Reading

TASK J

Der liebe Heinz

Heinz war mein Wunschkind. Als er geboren wurde, hatte ich schon eine 15jährige Tochter. Das war vor 13 Jahren. Das Mädchen ist schon mit 18 von zu Hause weggegangen. Mein Mann hat mich vier Jahre nach der Geburt meines Sohnes verlassen. Es bleibt mir nur Heinz.
Ich habe versucht, ihm die Liebe von Vater und Mutter zu geben.

„Du hast keine Freunde mehr. Deine ganze Freizeit gehört dem Jungen," sagt seine Tante zu mir. „Warum kann er das Wochenende nicht bei mir verbringen? Sein Freund kann auch mitkommen." Aber, ich habe Angst, wenn er nicht bei mir ist.

Als er noch klein war, brachte ich ihn jeden Morgen zur Schule. Wenn wir dort ankamen, begann er zu weinen. Er wollte in die Stadt gehen. Ich hatte kein Kindermädchen und ich mußte zur Arbeit gehen. Was sollte ich machen? Ich nahm ihn wieder nach Hause mit und meldete mich im Büro krank.

Jetzt meint sein Klassenlehrer: „Heinz will immer der Größte und der Beste sein, und wenn er es nicht schafft, schlägt er seine Klassenkameraden. Mit ihm haben sie alle die schlimmsten Probleme."

Computer-Spiele, eine Stereoanlage, ein Mountainbike mußte er unbedingt haben. Ich habe nie nein gesagt. Sein Zimmer sieht aus wie ein Spielzeugladen, aber er will nicht, daß seine Freunde mitspielen.

„Kinder essen, was auf den Tisch kommt!" meint meine Schwester. Aber mein Sohn ißt nur, was ihm schmeckt, soviel, daß ich zu ihm sage: „Jetzt hast du sicher keinen Hunger mehr." Danach kauft er aber Schokolade und Pommes. Kein Wunder, daß sein Taschengeld nicht reicht, obwohl er eine Menge hat.

Heinz kommt nach Hause, wann er will. Er redet kaum noch mit mir. Er schlägt seine Zimmertür zu und dreht die Musik laut auf. Ist das die Quittung für meine Liebe?

Was ist hier richtig? Kreuzen Sie das richtige Kästchen an.

1 Heinz ist

    A 4 Jahre alt. ☐

    B 13 Jahre alt. ☐

    C 15 Jahre alt. ☐

    D 18 Jahre alt. ☐ (1)

2 Heinz hat

    A keine Freunde. ☐

    B keine Geschwister. ☐

    C keine nahen Verwandten. ☐

    D keinen Vater. ☐ (1)

3 Anstatt in die Schule zu gehen,

    A blieb Heinz manchmal bei einem Kindermädchen. ☐

    B blieb Heinz manchmal zu Hause. ☐

    C ging Heinz manchmal in die Stadt. ☐

    D ging Heinz manchmal ins Büro seiner Mutter. ☐ (1)

Reading 3

4 In seiner Klasse ist Heinz immer

    A der Beste. ☐

    B der Freundlichste. ☐

    C der Größte. ☐

    D der Unfreundlichste. ☐ (1)

5 A Heinz bekommt von seiner Mutter immer, was er will. ☐

    B Einmal, als er etwas wollte, hat seine Mutter „nein" gesagt. ☐

    C Heinz hat so viele Spielzeuge, daß er sie seinen Freunden gibt. ☐

    D Heinz macht seine Spielzeuge kaputt. ☐ (1)

6 A Heinz hat oft keinen Hunger. ☐

    B Heinz ißt alles, was auf den Tisch kommt. ☐

    C Heinz ißt nur, was er will. ☐

    D Heinz kauft nie etwas zu essen. ☐ (1)

7 Heinz bekommt

    A kein Taschengeld, weil er einen Job hat. ☐

    B überhaupt kein Geld. ☐

    C viel Taschengeld. ☐

    D wenig Taschengeld. ☐ (1)

8 A Heinz kommt immer zur rechten Zeit nach Hause. ☐

    B Heinz spricht oft mit seiner Mutter. ☐

    C Heinz läßt seine Zimmertür immer offen. ☐

    D Heinz spielt laute Musik auf seinem Zimmer. ☐ (1)

Lesen Sie den folgenden Artikel, und beantworten Sie dann die Fragen auf deutsch.

TASK K

Ich hatte plötzlich Angst, als ich zwei Löschwagen im Wald sah. War denn ein Brand ausgebrochen? Wo? Ich brauchte nicht nervös zu sein. Mit dem Inhalt der Wagen wurden 10 000 neugepflanzte Bäume angegossen. Dann wuschen sich die Kinder der Waldjugend nach der Arbeit die Hände.

Die Freizeit dieser Kinder gehört dem Naturschutz. Sie machen die Waldränder wieder grün. Die meisten sind acht bis sechzehn Jahre alt. Zuerst müssen sie ein paar Stunden in der Forstschule verbringen, um etwas über die Wälder und Bäume zu lernen. Sie müssen auch die Vögel studieren. Nach den Gruppenstunden räumen sie im Wald auf – für zwei Wochen hat ihnen ein Bauer einen Traktor gegeben. Im Frühling kontrollieren und reparieren sie Nester, im Sommer zählen sie die Vögel, und jeden Herbst bauen sie Futterhäuschen.

Das älteste Mitglied Wolfgang sagt: „Meine Freunde sind alle im Sport- oder Musikverein, während ich meine Freizeit bei dem Naturschutz verbringe."

Seit fünfunddreißig Jahren gibt es die Waldjugend. Der Leiter dieser Gruppe, Klaus Huber (heute 75 Jahre alt – aber das glaubt ihm keiner), behauptet: „Heute sind die Kinder aktiv, deren Eltern damals als Kinder bei der Waldjugend mit mir die Natur erleben lernten."

3 Reading

1. Wozu brauchte man die Feuerwehrwagen im Wald?

   (i) .... (1)

   (ii) .... (1)

2. Wohin gehen die Kinder, um Naturschutz zu lernen?

   .... (1)

3. Was hat ein Bauer den Kindern geliehen, und wozu?

   .... (2)

4. Wie schützen die Kinder die Vögel?

   (a) im April: .... (1)

   (b) im Oktober: .... (1)

5. Laut Wolfgang, wofür interessieren sich seine Freunde?

   .... (1)

6. Was denkt man von dem Gruppenleiter nicht?

   .... (1)

7. Was haben die Eltern dieser Kinder schon gemacht?

   ....

   .... (2)

UCLES 1995

Reading 3

TASK L

Wählen Sie die passenden Namen.
Sie dürfen den selben Namen mehr als einmal schreiben.

Probleme mit dem Erwachsenwerden?

A Anja, 19:
Manchmal würde ich auch viel lieber Kind bleiben.

B Ogi, 12:
Als Erwachsener kann ich viele Dinge nicht mehr machen: mit meinen Flugzeugen spielen oder schnell rennen. Ich will immer klein bleiben.

C Suzanne, 17:
Mit 14 gab es immer Krach mit meinen Eltern, als ich weggehen wollte. Heute verstehe ich mich mit ihnen sehr gut, denn ich kann mit meinen Eltern über alle Probleme sprechen.

D Nicole, 17:
In manchen Dingen behandeln mich meine Eltern wie eine Erwachsene. Zum Beispiel, wenn ich Aufgaben erfüllen muss. Manchmal behandeln sie mich wie ein Kind, zum Beispiel, wenn ich am Wochenende ausgehen möchte.

E Marc, 16:
Gut finde ich, dass man mit 18 Auto fahren darf oder spät abends in Diskos gehen kann. Ich habe aber Angst davor, dass ich keine Stelle finde.

F Verena, 17:
Für mich war es schwierig, im Kreis meiner Freunde eine eigene Meinung zu haben. Jetzt habe ich die Chance, etwas allein zu machen und unabhängig zu werden.

G Kerstin, 15:
Mit meinen Eltern habe ich immer Krach, weil ich meine Kleider herumliegen lasse. Sie verstehen meine Probleme nicht. Zum Beispiel streiten wir uns, weil ich jetzt einen Freund habe und abends ausgehe.

BEISPIEL: Wer spielt gern mit Spielzeugen? .... *Ogi* ....

1 Welche Personen finden die Kindheit schön? ....und............. (2)

2 Wer hat Angst vor der Arbeitslosigkeit? .... (1)

3 Wer findet die Eltern manchmal tolerant, manchmal nicht? .... (1)

4 Wer kommt mit den Eltern jetzt gut aus? .... (1)

5 Welche Personen bekommen heute noch Schwierigkeiten, wenn sie ausgehen?

...........................und........................... (2)

6 Wer will einen eigenen Weg finden? .... (1)

7 Wer hat ein unordentliches Zimmer? .... (1)

MEG 1998

3 Reading

TASK M Taschengeld

> **JUDITH** bekommt von ihrer Oma 80 Mark Taschengeld und von ihren Eltern 20 Mark. Das ist mehr Geld als Stefan, Peter und Merle von ihren Eltern erhalten. „Stimmt", meint Judith, „aber dafür kaufe ich auch Klamotten und Schulsachen. Meine Eltern kaufen nur Kleidung, die ich unbedingt brauche." Judith arbeitet ab und zu in einem Café. Von dem dort verdienten Geld erfüllt sie sich persönliche Wünsche. Ihr größter Traum: „Mit viel Geld, würde ich eine Frankreichtour machen und die netten Leute besuchen, die ich dort kennengelernt habe."
>
> Schulsachen muß **PETER** nicht kaufen „Die bezahlen meine Eltern." Sein größter Wunsch: „Wenn ich viel Geld hätte, würde ich nach Australien oder Amerika auswandern. Und wenn ich Geld zu verschenken hätte, würden es Tierschutz- und Umweltorganisationen bekommen."
>
> **STEFAN** bekommt 50 Mark Taschengeld im Monat. Den Betrag findet er „in Ordnung", obwohl das Geld selten reicht. In den Ferien verdient Stefan etwas dazu. „Dann räume ich in einem Lebensmittelgeschäft Waren in Regale ein." Von seinem Taschengeld kauft Stefan Süßigkeiten, Musik-CDs, kleine Geschenke wie Notizbücher oder Stifte und Pflanzen.
>
> **MERLE** bekommt 50 Mark Taschengeld im Monat. „Bei mir ist das Geld immer sofort weg. Aber 50 Mark sind okay. Meinen Kindern würde ich auch nicht mehr Geld geben." Merle ist Musik-Fan und kauft von ihrem Taschengeld oft CDs. „Wenn ich viel Geld hätte, würde ich viele CDs kaufen und eine schöne Reise machen. Wahrscheinlich würde ich noch einen Teil des Geldes an Privatpersonen geben, die sich für hungerleidende Kinder einsetzen."

Beantworte die Fragen. Schreib einen Namen.
Beispiel: Wer bekommt 20 Mark von den Eltern?   *Judith*

1 Wer bekommt das meiste Taschengeld? .... (1)

2 Wer gibt das Geld sehr schnell aus? .... (1)

3 Wer war schon im Ausland? .... (1)

4 Wer hat keinen Teilzeitjob? .... (1)

5 Wer hilft in einem Laden? .... (1)

6 Wer möchte in einem anderen Land wohnen? .... (1)

7 Wer muß die meiste eigene Kleidung kaufen? .... (1)

8 Wer denkt nicht daran, anderen Leuten mit dem
   Taschengeld zu helfen? .... (1)

NEAB 1997

Reading 3

TASK N

Lies zuerst Ankes Brief.
Anke schreibt einen Brief an die *Vertrauenslehrerin** der Schule.
* *liaison teacher – a teacher who is to help pupils, to liaise between pupils and staff in case of any problems and often between pupils and parents.*

Liebe Frau Baumgartner,

ich habe da ein Problem. Wie Sie wissen, macht unsere Klasse zu Ostern einen Austausch mit einer Schule in England. Alle meine Freunde und Freundinnen machen mit, aber meine Eltern wollen mich nicht mitfahren lassen.

Sie sagen, wenn die Engländer nach Deutschland kommen, kann keiner bei uns übernachten, weil unsere Wohnung zu klein ist. Wir haben im Moment auch nicht so viel Geld, mein Vater ist nämlich seit ungefähr vier Monaten arbeitslos.

Auch sagen sie, daß ich es nicht verdient habe, nach England zu fahren, weil ich zu faul bin und deshalb meine Noten in der Schule nicht gut sind.

Das stimmt aber gar nicht. Ja, in Englisch habe ich nur eine „drei", aber deswegen möchte ich ja nach England fahren.

Ich habe meine Eltern gestern noch einmal gefragt und jetzt sagen sie, daß der Termin für den Austausch nicht gut paßt, weil wir zu Ostern als Familie ein paar Tage zu meinen Großeltern fahren wollen. Es ist immer stinklangweilig bei meinen Großeltern: ich würde lieber mit meinen Freunden zusammen sein. Ich finde, meine Eltern sind richtig gemein; sie wollen einfach nicht, daß ich Spaß in England haben kann. Können Sie als Vertrauenslehrerin mir helfen? Wie kann ich meine Eltern dazu bringen, daß ich doch nach England fahren kann?

Anke D (Klasse 10b)

Jetzt lies die Antwort.

Liebe Anke,

ich kann verstehen, daß Du verärgert bist, aber Du mußt fair bleiben. Ich glaube nicht, daß Deine Eltern einfach gemein sind. Es gibt sicher gute Gründe, warum sie Dich nicht fahren lassen wollen. Wenn Eure Wohnung klein ist und Dein Vater arbeitslos ist, mußt Du realistisch sein.

Es gibt aber vielleicht doch zwei Möglichkeiten:

Erstens mußt Du Deinem Klassenlehrer sagen, daß Du ein Mädchen als Austauschpartner haben mußt, dann kannst Du mit ihr Dein Zimmer teilen.

Zweitens, wenn Dein Vater noch ohne Arbeit ist, könnte Deine Familie vielleicht Geld für die Reisekosten von der Schule bekommen, aber Du mußt selbst den Direktor fragen.

Am besten ist es, wenn Du noch einmal mit Deinen Eltern sprichst. Du kannst ihnen auch sagen, daß sie mich anrufen können oder, wenn sie möchten, komme ich auch zu Euch und spreche mit Deinen Eltern.

J. Baumgartner

3 Reading

Beantworte jetzt die Fragen zum ersten Teil.
Kreuze ✗ an, was richtig ist. Achtung! Mehr als ein Kästchen kann richtig sein.

1 Anke ist unzufrieden, weil...
   (a) sie keinen Austausch zu Ostern machen darf. ❑
   (b) ihre Freunde und Freundinnen einen Austausch machen. ❑
   (c) ihre Eltern es ihr nicht erlauben, nach England zu fahren. ❑

2 Ankes Eltern denken, daß...
   (a) die Wohnung in England zu klein ist. ❑
   (b) ein Austausch im Moment zu teuer für sie ist. ❑
   (c) Anke zuerst einen Job finden muß. ❑

3 Ankes Eltern meinen auch, daß...
   (a) sie fleißiger in der Schule arbeiten muß. ❑
   (b) sie nicht genug Geld verdient. ❑
   (c) ihre Noten besser werden müssen. ❑

4 Anke kann nicht am Austausch teilnehmen, weil...
   (a) die Großmutter sie besuchen will. ❑
   (b) ihre Eltern Anke bei sich haben wollen. ❑
   (c) dann die ganze Familie zu den Großeltern fährt. ❑

Jetzt beantworte die Fragen zum zweiten Teil.
Welche Sätze sind richtig? Kreuze ✗ nur die richtigen Kästchen an.

5 Frau Baumgartner denkt auch, daß Ankes Eltern gemein sind. ❑

6 Frau Baumgartner denkt, daß Anke unrealistisch ist. ❑

7 Anke soll versuchen, ein Mädchen als Austauschpartner zu bekommen. ❑

8 Der Direktor gibt Anke bestimmt Geld für den Austausch. ❑

9 Frau Baumgartner hat vor, mit dem Direktor über Ankes Problem zu sprechen. ❑

10 Ankes Eltern sollen den Klassenlehrer anrufen. ❑

11 Anke soll wieder mit ihren Eltern sprechen. ❑

12 Die Eltern können Frau Baumgartner anrufen. ❑

(12)
SEG 1997

Writing 4

ASSESSMENT OBJECTIVES

REVISION SUMMARY

The GCSE Writing examination will test your ability to do the following, depending on the Examination Board for which you are entered, so check your syllabus:

1) Foundation
One or two tasks, requiring only single words and set phrases, from the following:
- make a list;
- make diary entries;
- complete a form.

Another task, using 30–40 words*, from the following:
- write a message;
- write a post card;
- write notes.

*Some Boards do not state the number of words, but the tasks they suggest would be of about this length.

2) Foundation and Higher
One task from the following:
- write an informal letter (possibly in reply to another);
- write a formal letter (possibly in reply to another);
- respond to or develop a stimulus in German or visual stimulus.

The number of words required varies from Board to Board.

3) Higher
One task from the following (possibly based on a stimulus):
- write an informal letter;
- write a formal letter;
- write a narrative, account, report or article;
- compose a story;
- devise publicity material.

The number of words required varies from Board to Board.

At all levels, the instructions for the tasks will be in German, as will most stimulus material, although material in English as well as visuals and pictures may also be used.

4) Coursework
As an alternative to taking the Writing paper, your centre may opt to do Coursework. All the above tasks are suitable for Coursework, as are the sample questions and exam practice questions printed later in this section. Your teacher will give you closer guidance on choice of task and how to tackle it, but you can use this book for advice and practice.

NOTE: all Boards allow the use of a dictionary for the Writing paper. MEG allows either a monolingual or a bilingual dictionary, whereas all other Boards specify a bilingual dictionary.

4 Writing

REVISION SUMMARY

EXAMINATION TECHNIQUE

1) Foundation
The essential requirement is to **communicate**, to get the whole message across as clearly and as accurately as possible.

How accurate must you be?
The acid test is that a native speaker can **understand** what you have written. Grammatical errors will be ignored, unless they prevent clear understanding.
   NOTE: WJEC/CCEA allow extra marks for accuracy and WJEC also takes into account the range of language.

2) Foundation and Higher/Higher levels
You must still **communicate** all the required points.
   You must keep to the number of words suggested on the paper.

How accurate must you be?
To achieve maximum marks, you need to be as **accurate** as possible. You should check your work thoroughly for any errors.

What about style?
Whilst not sacrificing accuracy, you should avoid being simple and repetitive. You must vary the structures and expressions, and if you want the top grade, you must be prepared to be ambitious and extend the topic.

WHAT TO REVISE FOR WRITING

As for Speaking, you need to develop your **active vocabulary and grammar**. Re-read the revision summary for Speaking before you read the rest of this section – it also contains some time expressions which are valuable for Writing.

The best way to test your **vocabulary and grammar** is to do some actual tasks, such as those in this book. Unless you put it into practice, you will not know how much has stuck in your mind. Ask your teacher politely to mark any extra written work you do and to give you some advice about how to improve it. Your teacher wants you to succeed. Ask your teacher for further revision guidance, if you feel in need of it.

You need to have a sound grasp of **word order** to write well, particularly at Higher level. Check the advice on this in the Revision summary in the Reading section.
To gain a better language mark, particulary above Foundation level (Grade E), you need to **vary the structure of your sentence**. There are various ways to do this:

- Start with a time expression:
  Heute nachmittag um vier Uhr zwanzig ist Onkel Dieter vorbeigekommen. (Task B)
  Gestern haben wir den Dom besichtigt. (Task C)
  Note that the main verb, here the auxiliary *ist/haben*, comes in the second position in the sentence (after the time expression).

- Start with a place expression:
  Hier ist nicht viel los. (Task D)
  In diesem Haus wurde ein alter Mann ermordet. (Task G)

- Other starting words
  Vielleicht gehen wir in eine Disco. (Task A)
  Leider ist das Wetter nicht so schön. (Task C)
  Plötzlich erschien eine weiße Gestalt in meinem Zimmer. (Task G)

Writing 4

REVISION SUMMARY

- Use infinitive clauses:
  um Tante Ilse zu besuchen. (Task B)
  Es ist immer ein schönes Gefühl, eine treue Freundin zu haben. (Task F)
  Note the position of the infinitive at the end of the clause with *zu* standing in front of it.
- Use dependent clauses. Some examples:
  Ich wohne in einem kleinen Ort, wo jeder sich kennt. (Task D)
  ... in der Großstadt, die etwa zwanzig Kilometer von hier liegt. (Task D)
  Or this sentence with a few clauses:
  Ich fühle mich besonders für diesen Job geeignet, weil ich nämlich vier jüngere Geschwister habe, auf die ich aufpassen muß, wenn meine Eltern abends ausgehen. (Task E)
  You will notice that the main verb comes at the end of each clause.

Before you attempt the examination practice tasks in this section, you should read the sample questions and answers together with the Examiner's commentary on each answer. These will provide you with specific revision hints and notes about common errors to avoid. You may find that the standard of some of the answers is rather high, but bear in mind that you will have a dictionary to help you and, if you are doing Coursework, more time available to write accurately (except for the task performed in controlled conditions).

When you have completed work on the sample questions and answers, try to do the practice tasks one by one, or pick out those on which you feel weaker. Be sure to read the Examiner's commentary before you write your answers. The number of words required varies from Board to Board. Therefore no word limit has been set for any examination practice task (Task H onwards). Follow the requirements of your own Board.

GENERAL REVISION CHECKLIST

- When revising nouns, check **gender** *der/die/das* and **plural**.
- Revise how the following are used and their **case endings**:
  the definite article *der/die/das/die* (Plural)
  the indefinite article *ein* and also *kein*
  possessive adjectives *mein/unser*, etc.
  demonstrative adjectives *dieser/jener/jeder/solcher*, etc.
  interrogative adjective *welcher*
  interrogative pronoun *wer*
  possessive pronouns *meiner/ihrer*, etc.
  personal pronouns *ich/du*, etc.
  reflexive pronouns *mich/sich*, etc.
  relative pronoun *der/die/das/die* (Plural)
  demonstrative pronoun *der/die/das/die* (Plural).
- Have another look at the comparison of adjectives and adverbs and at comparative constructions *kleiner als ich/nicht so groß wie du*, etc.
- Check **case endings** for adjectives; there are three tables of these.
- Relearn prepositions, their usage and their cases.
- Remember which verbs govern the dative case (*danken/helfen/folgen*, etc.).
- Go over all aspects of verbs including verb tenses and how these are formed. Don't forget imperative, passive, subjunctive.
  In particular, go through your tables of mixed and strong verbs.
- Revise numbers, dates, time and time expressions.
- Make sure you know negative expressions. See the Revision summary in the Listening section (page 20) for some advice on this.
- Reconsider German word order, a tricky but vital aspect. See the Revision summary in the Reading section (page 30) for some advice on this.

If you need to revise this subject more thoroughly, see the relevant topics in the *Letts* GCSE *German Study Guide*.

4 Writing

FOUNDATION AND HIGHER
TASK D

Informal letter

Sie suchen einen deutschen Briefpartner/eine deutsche Briefpartnerin.

> Anja, 16. Postfach 15 20 05 München. Ich suche eine Brieffreundin aus England. Ich mag Schwimmen, Tanzen, Kino und meine Hunde!

> Roland, 16. Postfach 25 46 Münster. Ich wünsche mir Briefkontakte aus England. Meine Hobbys: Radfahren, Fußball, Reisen.

Schreiben Sie einen Brief an Anja oder Roland.
Beschreiben Sie:
- Ihre Familie.
- Ihre Stadt/Ihr Dorf.

Geben Sie Information über Ihre Hobbys.
Stellen Sie ein paar Fragen an Anja/Roland.

ANSWER

> Lieber Roland,
> ich habe deine persönliche Annonce im Jugendmagazin Juma gelesen. Du hast nicht soviel von dich[1] selbst geschrieben. Hast Du Geschwister? Was sind Deine Eltern von Beruf? Gehst du gern in die[2] Schule?
> Nun noch kurz zu mir. Ich bin der Jungste[3] von drei Kinder[4]. Meine Schwester ist schon verheiratet und hat ein kleines Mädchen. Mein Bruder arbeitet auf einem Bauernhof – das wurde[5] mir nicht soviel Spaß machen. Meine Eltern sind beide berufstätig. Mein Vater ist Geschäftsmann und muss jeden Morgen[6] schon früh das Haus verlassen. Meine Mutter ist Lehrer[7] und unterrichtet Mathe und Deutsch an unserer[8] Dorfschule.
> Ich wohne in einem[8] kleinen Ort, wo jeder kennt sich.[9] Hier ist nicht viel los – nichts wird für Jugendliche angeboten.[10] Am Wochenende arbeite ich in einem Laden in der Großstadt, die etwa zwanzig Kilometer von hier liegt. Wenn ich die Zeit habe, ich[11] fahre gern mit dem Rad in die Stadt, oder ich spiele Fußball, so wie du.
> Ich freue mich auf deine Antwort,
> dein Brieffreund
> Kevin

Examiner's commentary

There is no word limit, but remember to check this and to obey any instruction. Kevin starts by asking some questions. You do not have to take the tasks in the order they are printed, but it is wise to tick them off as you do them.

1 *von* takes the dative, so *von dir*. Revise prepositions!
2 Note correct use of accusative for motion (see Task A Note **2**).
3 An Umlaut should be put on the comparative *(jünger)* and superlative *(der Jüngste)* of a number of adjectives of one syllable like *jung*. Check these!
4 See Note **1** about *von*. An *-n* is added to the dative plural of all nouns except those ending in *-n* or *-s,* so: *Kindern*.
5 Umlaut again: *wurde* is imperfect tense, whereas *würde* meaning 'would', conditional, is wanted here.
6 Note the correct use of the accusative for definite time: *jeden Morgen* (see task C Note **4**).
7 Remember to make male/female distinction. To form the feminine of a profession, add *-in* to the masculine, so: *Lehrerin*. Warning: some feminine forms need an Umlaut, e.g. *Ärztin*.
8 Note correct use of dative for position (see Task C Note **2**).
9 The verb should come last in the subordinate clause: *wo jeder sich kennt*.
10 *werden* is used here to form the passive. Note the past participle *(angeboten)* at the end of the clause. The meaning here is 'nothing is offered/made available'.
11 After a subordinate clause (here starting with *wenn*), the verb in the following main clause must come next in the sentence before its subject, so: *fahre ich gern...*

Writing 4

TASK E

Formal letter
Sie suchen einen Job in einem internationalen Kinderlager an der Nordsee. Schreiben Sie einen Bewerbungsbrief mit folgenden Informationen:
- Wie lange Sie arbeiten könnten.
- Ihre persönlichen Eigenschaften.
- Ihre praktischen Erfahrungen.
- Ihre Sprachkenntnisse.

Stellen Sie ein paar Fragen über den Job.

ANSWER

Sehr geehrte Damen und Herren,
wie ich aus der Stellenanzeige in der Norddeutschen Zeitung vom 1. Juni entnehmen kann, brauchen Sie[1] diesen Sommer eine Jugendliche im internationalen Kinderlager an der Nordsee. Ich möchte hiermit für diesen Job bewerben[2] und werde Ihnen deshalb etwas über mich erzählen.
Ich bin ein unternehmungslustiger, kontaktfreudiger und sehr geduldiger Mensch und treibe gern Sport. Ich bin sehr sprachbegabt und beherrsche schon drei Sprachen – meine Muttersprache (Englisch), Französisch und Deutsch. Nächstes Jahr werde ich auch Spanisch lernen.[3]
Ich fühle mich[4] besonders für diesen Job geeignet, weil ich nämlich vier jüngeren[5] Geschwister habe, auf die ich aufpassen muss, wenn meine Eltern abends ausgehen. Ich habe bereits als Berufspraktikum in einem Kindergarten ausgeholfen.[6]
Mit ein paar Kindern[7] habe ich auch Ausflüge untergenommen[8] und Geburtstagsfeiern veranstaltet.[9]
Im [10] Juli oder im [10] August konnte[11] ich Ihnen behilflich sein. Wenn Sie mich für diesen Job anstellen würden[11], würden[11] Sie mich bitte über weitere Einzelheiten, wie Arbeitszeiten und Bezahlung, informieren.
Mit freundlichen Grüßen[12]
Rachel Jones

Examiner's commentary A good answer covering all the set tasks with varied structures.
1 Note correct word order (see Task D Note **11**).
2 Learn reflexive verbs: *bewerben* is reflexive, so: *ich möchte mich bewerben* (see Note **4**).
3 *werden* is used here for the future tense with the infinitive at the end of the sentence.
4 Correct use of reflexive verb *sich fühlen*.
5 Adjective ending: it should be *vier jüngere*.
6 Correct past participle of a separable verb – note the position of *-ge-*.
7 Correct dative plural of noun with *-n* ending (see Task D Note **4**); *mit* takes the dative.
8 *unternehmen* is inseparable, so: *unternommen*. Learn which verbs are inseparable!
9 If the verb starts with one of these inseparable prefixes: *be-, emp-, ent-, er-, ge-, miß-, ver-, zer-*, you do **not** add *ge-* to form the past participle.
10 *im* with months (*am* with days/parts of the day – *am Montag/am Nachmittag*; *um* with clock time – *um ein Uhr*).
11 Umlaut problem again: *konnte* is imperfect tense. You want *könnte* – conditional. Note correct conditional later: *würden* (see Task D Note **5**).
12 Note the most commonly used ending for a formal letter.

4 Writing

HIGHER

TASK F
Newspaper article

Die Schülerzeitung Ihrer deutschen Partnerschule sucht Artikel über "Freundschaft". Schreiben Sie einen Artikel darüber, indem sie erklären, was für Eigenschaften ein bester Freund/eine beste Freundin haben sollte.

ANSWER

Es ist immer ein schönes Gefühl, eine treue Freundin zu haben.[1] Man fühlt sich geliebt und geachtet. Wenn man Probleme bekommt, kann man sicher sein, dass man nicht allein dasteht.[2] Eine gute Freundin soll immer bereit sein, zu helfen.

Freunde kommen nicht aus dem Himmel geflogen. Eine Freundschaft entsteht nicht so einfach! Man muss sich zuerst eine Freundin aussuchen. Dann muss man Zeit füreinander haben.

Meiner besten[3] Freundin kann ich alles erzählen. Wenn es etwas ziemlich Doof[4] ist, wird sie mich nicht auslachen. Sie weiß alles über mich, auch meine tiefsten Geheimnisse. Die Tatsache, dass wir dieselben Interessen haben, bringt uns noch näher zusammen.

Sie ist immer offen, freundlich und hilfsbereit. Ab und zu gibt es zwischen uns kleine Mißverständnisse, aber die meiste Zeit verstehen wir uns sehr gut. Wir haben uns nur einmal gestreitet[5] – wegen einen[6] Junge[7] natürlich. Aber das war schnell vorbei.

Examiner's commentary An effective answer portraying the friend's character and conveying feelings.
1 Note correct infinitive phrase.
2 Spot the correct subordinate clauses in this sentence.
3 Correct use of dative *meiner* and appropriate adjective ending *besten*.
4 The adjective following *etwas* must begin with a capital letter and end in -*es*: *etwas Doofes*.
5 Revise the table of strong and mixed verbs! Write here: *gestritten*.
6 *wegen* takes the genitive, so: *wegen eines...*
7 Write here: *Jungen*. *Der Junge* is a weak masculine noun: -*(e)n* is added to these nouns in all cases except nominative singular. Look these up!

TASK G
Narrative

„Mitten in der Nacht hörte ich ein lautes Klopfen an der Haustür..." Erzählen Sie weiter.

ANSWER

Unsere Eltern waren fürs Wochenende weggefahren, und meine Freunde und ich hatten uns einen Gespensterfilm angesehen. Ich horchte wieder... Nichts. Dann hörte ich einen langen grollenden Donner. Ein schweres Gewitter kam[1] näher... Ich versuchte wieder einzuschlafen[2]. Ein wilder Schrei unterbrach[1] die Stille des Hauses. Sofort erinnerte ich mich an die Geschichte, die mir meine Mutter vor Jahren erzählt hatte. In diesem Haus wurde[1] ein alter Mann ermordet. Jedes Jahr an seinem Todestag soll sein Geist im Haus umgehen. Ich wusste[1] nicht mehr, wann[3] er gestorben[1] war.

Dann geschah[1] es zum zweiten Mal: dieser schrecklicher Schrei. Obwohl die Tür meines Schlafzimmers langsam sich[4] öffnete, kam[1] niemand herein. Ich wollte davonrennen, aber ich konnte mich nicht bewegen, weil mein ganzer Körper steif geworden[1] war. Kalter Angstschweiß stand[1] mir auf der Stirn.

Plötzlich erschien[1] eine weiße Gestalt in meinem Zimmer... sie trat[1] näher an mich heran[5]. Als[6] sie eine Hand erhob[1], schrie[1] ich:

"Nein, bitte... Was wollen Sie von mir? Bitte! Tun Sie's nicht!"

"Du hast einen richtigen Schreck bekommen![1] Bin aber kein Gespenst." Da stand[1] mein Freund Karl vor mir. Er hatte zwei Löcher in sein Bettlaken gerissen[1] und es über seinen Kopf gezogen.[1]

Writing 4

Examiner's commentary An interesting answer with a wide range of vocabulary and structure.
1 The imperfect and perfect tenses of weak verbs are easy to form: *hören – hörte – gehört*. However, you need to learn the table of strong and mixed verbs – if there is a vowel change from the infinitive when these verbs are used in this answer, this is shown by the note **1**.
2 Correct use of *zu* with the infinitive of a separable verb.
3 *wann* is used for direct or indirect questions.
4 Wrong position of *sich*: it should come after a subordinating conjunction, e.g. *obwohl*, in other words before the subject if it is a name or a noun, so: *Obwohl sich die Tür...* However, if the subject is a pronoun, it always comes before *sich*, even in subordinate clauses, e.g.: *Obwohl er sich nicht daran erinnerte...*
5 Correct position of separable prefix in simple tenses (present, imperfect) is, as here, on its own at end of the clause. In compound tenses, the whole of the separable verb comes at the end of the clause. In the future or conditional tenses and also after modal verbs and *lassen*, it is in the infinitive form: *ich werde ausgehen/ich will ausgehen*, but note its formation in infinitive phrases with *zu*: *ich hoffe, auszugehen*. In the perfect and pluperfect, it is in the form of a past participle: *ich bin gestern abend ausgegangen* – see Task E Note **6**.
6 Note the use of *als* to convey a single event (or state) in the past.

PART 2: EXAMINATION PRACTICE

FOUNDATION

TASK H

You are looking for a holiday job in Germany.
Schreib eine Karte **auf Deutsch**.
Du mußt folgende Informationen geben.
Student(in) sucht Ferienjob.

Ich suche einen Ferienjob	
Beispiel: Wie alt du bist	• *Ich bin sechzehn Jahre alt.*
Wie dein Charakter ist	• ....
Was für Hobbys du hast	• ....
Wie lange du schon Deutsch lernst	• ....
Welche Arbeit du machen möchtest	• ....
Wann du arbeiten kannst	• ....

Examiner's tip In spite of the example given, you do not need to write in sentences. The task is to convey the message clearly. Five simple but adequate answers are: *freundlich*; *Schwimmen und Malen*; *3 Jahre*; (*als*) *Kellner*; *im August*.

NEAB 1998

TASK I

Du fragst deine Freunde/Freundinnen, was sie in ihrer Freizeit machen. Schreibe ihre Antworten in ganzen Sätzen. Schreibe fünf Sätze.
   Beispiel: Meike spielt gern Hockey.

Examiner's tip Remember to use a sentence for each person, as in the example, and not to use any hobby more than once.

4 Writing

TASK J

Du verbringst eine Woche bei deinem Austauschpartner/deiner Austauschpartnerin in der Schweiz. Du hast schon ein paar Notizen gemacht. Schreibe jetzt für jeden Tag einen Satz in dein Tagebuch. Vorsicht – heute ist Dienstag!

Beispiel:
So: ANKUNFT
Antwort: Wir sind heute um siebzehn Uhr angekommen.

    Mo: (GESTERN) SCHULE – Besuch, aber keinen Unterricht

    ....

    Di: (HEUTE) STADTBESICHTIGUNG

    ....

    Mi: (MORGEN) AUSFLUG

    ....

    Do: SCHULE – Unterricht!

    ....

    Fr: EINKAUFEN

    ....

    Sa: DISCO

    ....

Examiner's tip You need to know the abbreviations for the days of the week. See Task A for the way to tackle this task, but you must follow here the indications for each day, e.g. *SCHULE – Besuch, aber keinen Unterricht.* There is no point in mentioning lessons, since you did not attend any, but you must include them on Thursday. For Monday you could write simply: *Heute haben wir unsere Partnerschule besucht.*

TASK K

Sie machen Ihr Berufspraktikum bei einer deutschen Firma. Herr Schmidt ruft an, und Sie nehmen den Hörer ab. Zuerst machen Sie folgende Notizen:

Herr Schmidt – Krankheit
Termin heute bei Frau Halle – X Entschuldigung
vielleicht nächste Woche?
bitte unser neues Produkt schicken

Jetzt schreiben Sie eine Nachricht an die Verkaufsleiterin, Frau Halle.

Examiner's tip You can make use of the notes, but you need to build them into sentences of your own making, sometimes altering the words given, e.g.: *Herr Schmidt ist krank. Er hat heute einen Termin bei Frau Halle, aber (er entschuldigt sich) er kann nicht kommen.* The words in brackets can be left out.

Writing 4

FOUNDATION AND HIGHER

TASK L

Dein Brieffreund/Deine Brieffreundin will dich in den Sommerferien besuchen. Schreibe einen Brief mit folgenden Informationen bzw. Fragen:

- Wann, wie lange.
- Wie du ihn/sie abholst.
- Sein/ihr Schlafzimmer.
- Aktivitäten/Ausflüge usw.
- Essen.

Examiner's tip See Task D for an informal letter pattern. *bzw. = beziehungsweise* = or. You can either provide information to your penfriend **or** ask him/her questions about any of the items listed. For example:
either: *Wann möchtest Du kommen, und wie lange könntest Du bleiben?*
or: *Du könntest im August kommen und den ganzen Monat bleiben, wenn Du willst.*
Try to include a few questions, rather than merely giving information.

TASK M

Du fährst nächsten Monat nach Deutschland, und dein(e) Brieffreund(in) hat dir diesen Brief geschickt. Beantworte den Brief!

> Hagen, den 4. Juni
>
> Hallo!
>
> Wann und wie kommst Du nach Deutschland? Wo sollen wir Dich abholen? Mein Vater fragt, was Du gern machen möchtest, während Du hier bist.
>
> Was machst Du eigentlich am liebsten in Deiner Freizeit? Ich möchte Deinen Aufenthalt bei uns ein bißchen planen. Ich habe einen neuen Computer. Magst Du gern Computerspiele?
>
> Was hast Du in den letzten Tagen gemacht? Ist das Wetter bei Euch so schlecht wie hier - jeden Tag Regen?
>
> Kannst Du mir bitte etwas aus England für meinen jüngeren Bruder mitbringen - ein Fußballhemd von Manchester United?
>
> Tschüß und bis nächsten Monat!
>
> Deine
>
> Helga

Dein Brief soll wie ein richtiger Brief beginnen und enden.
Schreib 100 bis 120 Wörter.

Examiner's tip The instructions tell you that you must write a proper letter with correct beginning and ending. You should make sure you answer all Helga's questions: there are 7 direct ones indicated by question marks, but can you spot the indirect one? If you have words left, ask her some questions without copying hers.

SEG 1997

4 Writing

TASK N Lies diese Kleinanzeige:

> JUGENDHERBERGE
>
> EICHBORN
>
> sucht
>
> junge Leute,
>
> die im Sommer
>
> in unserer Jugendherberge
>
> arbeiten können.
>
> Sprachkenntnisse erwünscht.

Schreib einen Brief an die Jugendherberge Eichborn!
Beginne und ende den Brief richtig!

Schreib
- wer du bist.
- wie lange du schon Deutsch lernst.
- warum du die Stelle möchtest.
- über dein Berufspraktikum oder deinen Samstagjob.

Stell fragen
- über die Arbeitsstunden.
- wievel Geld du bekommen wirst.

> **Examiner's tip** Make sure you write a formal letter (see task E) covering all the bullet points. Emphasise your knowledge of German and of any other foreign language(s). You may write about your own part-time job and work experience, but if you are confident of your German, you can make up work experience which suits this job in a youth hostel.

WJEC 1998

TASK O Sie sehen nicht oft fern, weil Sie die meisten Sendungen uninteressant finden. Schreiben sie einen Brief an ein deutsches Fersehmagazin, in dem Sie sich über die englischen Sendungen beklagen und bessere Programme vorschlagen.

> **Examiner's tip** You can concentrate on television in your country. You are not expected to have any knowledge of German television, but if you do, you should mention any programmes which seem interesting. Try not to overuse any item of vocabulary. Some ways of conveying boredom, apart from *langweilig*, are: *uninteressant* (as in question wording), *ohne Interesse, monoton, sich langweilen, Langeweile haben, bei einer Sendung fast einschlafen*. You should also make positive suggestions about the type of programme you wish to see.

Writing 4

TASK P

Ihr Freund/Ihre Freundin hat Probleme mit den Eltern. Schreiben Sie einen Brief an die Kummerkastentante eines deutschen Jugendmagazins.

- Erklären sie das Problem.
- Sagen Sie, was Sie davon halten.
- Bitten Sie um Rat.

Examiner's tip — die Kummerkastentante = agony aunt (who will give advice – *Rat* – about problems). Keep to a topic for which you know most of the vocabulary. You don't want to spend too much time looking up words in your dictionary. Don't forget to ask for advice and to give your own opinions.

HIGHER

TASK Q

Ihre deutsche Partnerstadt/Ihr deutsches Partnerdorf bereitet eine Broschüre über Ihre Stadt/Ihr Dorf vor. Sie wollen über die folgenden Aspekte schreiben:

- eine kurze Geschichte der Stadt/des Dorfes.
- die Stadt/das Dorf heute – Probleme?
- wie Sie sich die Zukunft der Stadt/des Dorfes vorstellen.

Examiner's tip — At Higher level, you will have to be proficient in your use of tenses and show imagination. See if you can do so here.

TASK R

Sie sind mit Ihrer Familie auf Urlaub in Österreich. Jemand ist in Ihre Ferienwohnung eingebrochen. Schreiben Sie einen Bericht für die Polizei, in dem Sie folgendes erwähnen:

- Wann es passiert ist.
- Wo Sie zu der Zeit waren.
- Schäden.
- Was gestohlen wurde – Wert und genaue Beschreibung.
- Zeugen – ob jemand etwas gesehen hat.

Examiner's tip — A task combining narrative and description. Make sure you cover all the points listed. Avoid writing too many words when giving details of the stolen articles. You should try to mention your feelings and you could possibly comment on the number of crimes committed today.

TASK S

Ein deutsches Jugendmagazin sucht Artikel über:

- entweder die Gefahren des Rauchens
- oder die Gefahren des Alkohols.

Schreiben Sie einen Artikel.

Examiner's tip — Listen again to the Presentation and Discussion on the CD together with the Examiner's commentary in the Speaking section of this book, in order to revise some of the necessary vocabulary.

4 Writing

TASK T

Was würde Ihr Traumberuf sein? Erzählen Sie davon, indem Sie folgendes erwähnen:

- Was Sie machen würden, und warum es Ihnen gefallen würde.
- Ihren Lohn, und wofür Sie das Geld ausgeben würden.
- Ihre idealen Arbeitskollegen/-kolleginnen.
- Einen Nachteil dieses Berufs.

> **Examiner's tip** You need to use the conditional tense with *würde*, as in the first two sub-tasks. Remember to discuss one negative aspect, as indicated in the last sub-task *(Nachteil)*.

TASK U

Sie wollen an einem Preisausschreiben in der Schülerzeitung Ihrer deutschen Partnerschule teilnehmen. Der Artikel heißt: „Die ideale Schule". Erwähnen Sie in Ihrem Artikel:

- Fächer und Lehrer.
- Hausaufgaben, Klassenarbeiten, Prüfungen.
- Schuluniform.
- Schulordnung.
- Schülervertretung (SMV).

> **Examiner's tip** *Schülervertretung (SMV)* = school council, on which a representative of each class sits.
> Get rid of/abolish = *etwas* (accusative) *loswerden/abschaffen*, or *keine Schuluniform haben*.
> It is up to you to be humorous or serious in tone in this task. Try to give reasons for your opinions.

TASK V

Beschreiben Sie Ihren Lieblingsstar – Fernsehstar, Schauspieler(in), Sportler(in), oder Sänger(in).
    Erwähnen Sie:

- Persönlichkeit.
- Leistungen.
- Warum Sie ihn/sie bewundern.

> **Examiner's tip** The third sub-task is linked to the first two. You must give your own opinions instead of doing a mere biography or character sketch.

TASK W

Schreiben Sie eine Kritik von einem Film, den Sie neulich gesehen haben. Erwähnen Sie:

- Handlung.
- Charaktere und ihre Eigenschaften.
- Schauspieler(innen).
- Ob Ihnen der Film gefallen hat, und warum/warum nicht.

Writing 4

Examiner's tip Again your own views are being sought. Imagine you are writing the film review for a group of German teenagers and explain why they should or should not see the film.

Gestern war Ihr Unglückstag. Erzählen Sie, warum.

TASK X

Examiner's tip If there is an alternative, don't attempt such a task, unless you have a good imagination. You are given no help with the content. As you will see in many of these Higher tasks, you need to show your feelings about the various things that happened.

Wir waren immer noch hoch oben auf dem Berg, als die Sonne unterging... Erzählen Sie weiter.

TASK Y

Examiner's tip See tip for Task X. You should explain why you were still on the mountain so late in the day and how you eventually came down. Apart from telling a coherent story, you ought to include some description and write about your feelings.

Erzählen Sie die folgende Geschichte.

TASK Z

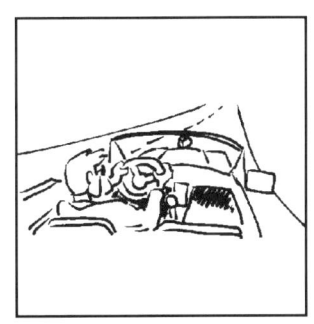

Examiner's tip The pictures allow for both story telling and description. You should show the man's feelings at the different stages of the story.

5 Mock examination paper

QUESTIONS

There now follows a full sample Higher examination in Speaking, Reading and Writing which gives you some extra material to practise prior to taking your exam for real in the summer.

After the exam papers, answers are given to the Reading paper with some indication of how different marks would convert to different grades. However, you must remember that your final grade is based on your performance in all four skills. There are no 'correct answers' to the Writing and Speaking papers. The answers you give on these papers would have to be marked by an experienced teacher or examiner. So instead of answers, some notes are given.

The papers are of Higher tier standard. They use different types of exercises that may be used by any Examination Board.

READING

Time allowed: 50 minutes   You may use a dictionary.   Answer all questions.

AUFGABE 1

Hotel Waldheim
Ruhige Lage. Freibad. Vollpension. Komfortable Zimmer mit Bad, Balkon. Herrliche Wanderwege. Bitte verlangen Sie die Preisliste.

Pension Fischer
Neu renoviertes Haus in zentraler Lage. Nähe Einkaufszentrum. Alle Zimmer mit Dusche. Zum Teil mit Balkon. Fernsehraum. Vollpension.

Hotel-Restaurant Sonnenberg
Absolut ruhige Lage direkt am Rande der Natur. Tausend Möglichkeiten für Wanderungen und Ausflüge. Alle Zimmer haben Bäder und Kabelfernsehen.

Gästehaus Eckert
Im Stadtzentrum gegenüber Bahnhof. Zimmer ohne Bad/Dusche. Keine Haustiere. Frühstücksbuffet, Mittagessen, Abendtisch. Sonderpreise Früh- und Spätsaison.

Hotel-Wirtshaus Krone
Am Stadtrand. Spazierwege am Haus. Alle Mahlzeiten. Aufenthaltsraum mit Farb-TV. Unser Hausprospekt informiert Sie ausführlich.

	🛁	🚿	📺	🍴	🛏	🚶	Stadtmitte
Waldheim	✔		✔	✔	✔		
Fischer							
Sonnenberg							
Eckert							
Krone							

AUFGABE 2 (6)

Holiday advertisements

A Urlaub für die ganze Familie. Jüngere Kinder bleiben im Strandklub, während Eltern die Stadt besichtigen oder Jugendliche Wasserski laufen oder einkaufen gehen.

B Gesundheitszentrum im Naturpark. Familienspaß mit Sport und Wanderungen – oder nehmen Sie den Donau-Radweg. Aktivitäten den ganzen Tag. Abends zum Relaxen.

64

C Versuchen Sie unsere neue 18-Loch Golfanlage. Zusatzprogramm für Kinder mit Ponyreiten und Malstunden im Naturgebiet. Abends ist auch viel los! Babysitten kostenlos!

D Genießen Sie 7 Tage mit viel Kultur: Besuch in Museen, Schlossbesichtigung, Theater, Oper.

E Skischule mit geprüften Lehrern und dem Schwarzwaldmeister bietet Stunden für alle, auch für Kinder ab 3 Jahren. Dazu noch Eislaufen und Eis-Disco, Pferde- und Rodelschlitten.

Which holiday best suits which family?

1 Children like horseriding and painting, parents want to go out on their own in the evening. (1)

2 The whole family wants a wintersports holiday. (1)

3 Family needs plenty of daytime activity to keep fit and to tire the children out, so parents can have a quiet evening. (1)

4 Young children love a sea-side holiday, but older children and parents need other distractions. (1)

AUFGABE 3

Jazz auf hoher See

Zweieinhalb Tage können Sie an Bord von „M/S Prinzessin Stephanie" Dixieland-Jazz non-stop genießen. Von Kiel aus reisen Sie für nur 199 DM nach Oslo und zurück, mit viel Musik, skandinavischem Buffet und netten Leuten. Natürlich ist auch ein Bummel durch das Einkaufszentrum in der norwegischen Hauptstadt geplant. Stadtrundfahrt mit Zuschlag.

Welche Sätze sind richtig? Kreuzen Sie nur 3 Kästchen an.

Beispiel: Man macht Urlaub an Bord eines Schiffes. ☑

    Man macht eine Reise mit dem Zug. ☐

A Man verbringt 2 halbe Tage an Bord des Schiffes. ☐

B An Bord kann man die ganze Zeit Jazz hören. ☐

C Die Fahrt beginnt in Oslo. ☐

D An Bord gibt es kein deutsches Essen. ☐

E Man kann in Norwegen einkaufen gehen. ☐

F Eine Stadtrundfahrt ist im Preis inbegriffen. ☐ (3)

Mock examination paper

QUESTIONS

AUFGABE 4

Die erste Arbeitsstelle

Im Arbeitsamt hat ihr der Chef einer großen Firma seine Visitenkarte zugesteckt. „Wenn Sie einen Arbeitsplatz suchen, rufen Sie mich an." Kürzere Zeit später hatte Heike den ersten Arbeitsvertrag unterschrieben. Die 21jährige arbeitet bei einem Unternehmen, das Telefonleitungen überprüft. Bei Fehlern im Netz muss sic sogar nachts zur Stelle sein.

Bei der Firma gibt es Ausbildungsplätze sowohl für Haupt- und Realschüler als auch für Gymnasiasten. „Mit dem, was die Azubis hier lernen, haben sie bessere Chancen, eine Stelle zu finden als in anderen Berufen", meint Heike. „Es ist echt toll – man arbeitet mit der Zukunftstechnologie. Alles hat sich in der Elektronik in den letzten 30 Jahren geändert."

Der Chef sagt: „Fast alle Mädchen, die hier arbeiten oder sich ausbilden, wollen später den Elektrobetrieb von Papa übernehmen. Aber Heikes Vater ist Briefträger!"

Kreuzen Sie an, ob die Sätze falsch oder richtig sind.   Falsch   Richtig

1 Heike hat den Chef einer großen Firma besucht.   ☐   ☐   (1)

2 Später hat der Chef Heike angerufen.   ☐   ☐   (1)

3 Heike muß das Telefonnetz reparieren.   ☐   ☐   (1)

4 Man muß auf einem Gymnasium sein, um einen
   Ausbildungsplatz zu bekommen.   ☐   ☐   (1)

5 Man hat bessere Chancen in anderen Berufen als
   in der Elektronik.   ☐   ☐   (1)

6 In der Elektronik ist es jetzt nicht mehr so wie vor
   dreißig Jahren.   ☐   ☐   (1)

7 Die meisten Frauen in der Elektronik möchten im
   Familienbetrieb arbeiten.   ☐   ☐   (1)

AUFGABE 5

Mein Sohn ist ein Dieb

Liebe Tante Dora!

Bis vor einem Jahr war mein Sohn Martin ein braver Junge, sogar ein Musterkind. Doch auf einmal wird er immer frecher, und was mich besonders beunruhigt: Er klaut mir Geld. Letzten Monat habe ich bemerkt, dass in meinem Portemonnaie ein Zwanziger fehlte. Ich fand den Schein später in seiner Hosentasche. Seitdem hat mir Geld schon öfter gefehlt. Warum tut er das? Er kriegt doch sechs Mark Taschengeld die Woche, und er ist erst zehn Jahre alt. Ist das zuwenig?

Isabell

Liebe Isabell!

Sechs Mark pro Woche sind für einen Zehnjährigen nicht genug. Das sind ungefähr fünfundzwanzig Mark im Monat. Üblich sind mindestens fünfunddreißig Mark. Sprich sofort mit Martin. Wenn du ihm nichts sagst, wird er weiterstehlen. Auf Strafen wird er böse reagieren. Sei nett zu ihm!

Tante Dora

Mock examination paper 5

QUESTIONS

Wähhlen Sie die Antwort, die am besten passt. Dann füllen Sie die Lücken aus.

1   Letztes Jahr war Martin .... (1)
    ein frecher Junge   *ein guter Junge*   *ein unruhiger Junge*

2   Er nimmt Geld .... seiner Mutter. (1)
    aus dem Portemonnaie   *aus der Tasche*   *aus dem Bankkonto*

3   Letzten Monat hat er ....genommen. (1)
    DM 6   *DM 20*   *DM 30*

4   Er hat .... Geld genommen. (1)
    nur einmal   *jeden Monat*   *oft*

5   Normalerweise bekommt ein Zehnjähriger .... Taschengeld im Monat. (1)
    DM 6   *DM 25*   *DM 35*

6   Martins Mutter sollte .... (1)
    mit ihm reden   *ihm nichts sagen*   *ihn bestrafen*

AUFGABE 6

Eine junge Türkin in Deutschland

Dilaras Familie kommt aus der Türkei. Als sie alle nach Deutschland umgezogen sind, war Dilara noch ziemlich jung. Aber an die ersten Tage hier kann sie sich noch klar erinnern. Alles war ihr fremd. Die Nachbarn waren nicht froh, dass Ausländer neben ihnen wohnten. Sie konnten die türkische Familie zuerst nicht verstehen, weil ihre Sitten und Gebräuche ganz anders waren.

In der Schule hatte Dilara riesige Probleme – nicht nur wegen der Sprache. Während der Pausen blieb sie immer allein. Die anderen Schülerinnen machten sich über sie lustig. Aber jetzt hat sie in ihrer Klasse neue Freunde kennengelernt, die sie als Deutsche akzeptieren, „obwohl ich nicht versuche, so wie sie zu sein", behauptet sie. Sie will hier in der Schule weiterlernen und dann auf der Uni studieren. Sie möchte einen guten Beruf erlernen – „Anwältin oder Ärztin, das wäre sehr schön", sagt sie.

Sie muss aber anerkennen, dass es für eine Türkin nicht leicht ist, eine gute Arbeitsstelle zu finden. Ihre Eltern meinen, sie soll zu Hause bleiben, um ihre kleineren Geschwister zu versorgen, weil das eben die Rolle einer Frau ist. Die Arbeitgeber haben Angst vor Fremden. „Sie würden vielleicht glauben, dass ich nur zu einer niedrigeren Arbeit geeignet sei", erklärt sie.

Beantworten Sie die Fragen auf Deutsch.

1   Was hat ihre Familie gemacht, als Dilara jung war?

    .... (1)

2   Wie fühlte sich Dilara zu dieser Zeit?

    .... (1)

5 Mock examination paper

QUESTIONS

3 Worüber ärgerten sich die Nachbarn?

....

.... (2)

4 Welche Probleme hatte Dilara in der Schule?

....

....

.... (3)

5 Was meinen ihre Klassenkameradinnen jetzt von ihr?

.... (1)

6 Was sind ihre Zukunftspläne?

....

....

.... (3)

7 Was meinen ihre Eltern dazu?

....

.... (2)

8 Laut Dilara, was halten die Arbeitgeber von Fremden?

.... (1)

WRITING

Time allowed: 1 hour. You may use a dictionary. Answer both questions.

1 Dein neuer deutscher Freund/deine neue deutsche Freundin kommt im August nach England. Schreib ihm/ihr einen Brief auf Deutsch.
Gib Informationen über: deine Stadt/die nächste Stadt; Aktivitäten im August; deine Osterferien. Frag ihn/sie über: seine/ihre Schule; seine/ihre Freizeit.

2 Sie waren Zeuge/Zeugin eines Unfalls. Schreiben Sie einen Bericht für die Polizei. Erwähnen Sie folgendes: was passiert ist; Reaktionen der Fahrer und der Passanten; Ihre Meinung über den Unfall.

Mock examination paper 5

SPEAKING

QUESTIONS

You have 15 minutes to prepare the three sections below.

SECTION 1
You would like a job in a restaurant. You go to meet the manager. He/she starts the conversation.
1 Give your name and surname. Say how to spell them.
2 Say what job you would like.
3 Explain what you did in your last job in a hotel.
4 Ask about working hours and days.
5 Answer the manager's question (!)

1 Name und Vorname 2 Arbeit im Restaurant 3 Job im Hotel 4 Wann? 5 !

(The examiner's roles can be played by a friend who speaks German.)
Examiner's role (The number at the end of a line shows the candidate's next task.)
Sie beginnen.
Guten Morgen. Wie heißen Sie? (Wie schreibt man das?) (1)
Was für eine Arbeit möchten Sie hier machen? (2)
Was haben Sie bei Ihrem letzten Job gemacht? (3)
Das hört sich alles sehr interessant an. (4)
Dienstags bis samstags, 12.00 – 22.00. Aber warum wollen Sie in einem deutschen Restaurant arbeiten? (5)

SECTION 2
CAMPING AM TITISEE

Examiner's role

Wo haben Sie die Ferien verbracht?

Was haben Sie dort gemacht? Tagsüber? Abends?

Was haben Sie gegessen?

Wie war das Wetter? Probleme?

SECTION 3
Sprechen Sie über diese drei Themen:
A Ihre Hobbys *B* Ihre Weihnachtsferien *C* Ihre Zukunftspläne.

Answers

This section provides answers for the Listening and Reading exercises in this book. Please note that in the case of some Listening tasks, insufficient or imprecise answers are included in italics after the genuine answers. These italicised answers highlight the traps that candidates frequently fall into when they try to guess the answer, not having fully understood what they have listened to.

LISTENING ANSWERS

Task	Answer	Mark
A	C	1

> **Examiner's tip** All three ways of going to town shown in the pictures are mentioned in the dialogue, so you have to eliminate two of them. The objection to A is that it is *zu weit* and, as said at the end, *zu anstrengend* ('too tiring').
> Even if you did not know *anstrengend*, you should be familiar with *weit*, although many candidates forget it in the Speaking test. Your friend's mother has to go to work with the car, so you can't have a lift: the words *leider nicht* ('unfortunately not') in the friend's statement indicates that this solution won't work. Little words such as this can be crucial for your understanding. Just because the idea of walking is mentioned last, don't assume that it must be the answer!

Task	Answer	Mark
B 1	B	1
2	D	1

> **Examiner's tip** Knowledge of directions should provide you with some easy marks, but candidates often confuse *Kreuzung* ('crossroads') with *Ampel* ('traffic light'). Surprisingly, ordinal numbers *erste(r)*, *zweite(r)*, *dritte(r)*, etc. are sometimes poorly learnt. Some candidates also have little sense of left and right. If you had any trouble at all in this task, revise directions thoroughly.

Task	Answer	Mark
C 1	B	1
2	A	1

> **Examiner's tip** Numbers are essential for this task but are often poorly revised. It is important to practice hearing them, so say them aloud when you look them up in future. When you hear them in 24-hour times, listen out for the word *Uhr* which comes in between the number for the hour and the number for the minutes, e.g. *sieben Uhr dreißig*. This helps you to separate and work out the two numbers.
> **1** *verpassen* = to miss, so you can ignore the 7.00 train.
> **2** *Wo?* can be used to mean *auf welchem Gleis?*, 'from which platform?'.

Listening answers

Task		Answer	Mark
D	1	2nd floor (im zweiten Stock – 2)	1
	2	Ground (im Erdgeschoß – E)	1
	3	1st floor (im ersten Stock – 1)	1
	4	2nd floor (2)	1
	5	Ground (E)	1

Examiner's tip   A short piece to listen to is not always easy, particularly if it is a monologue. Quite a few details need to be grasped in a short period of time. Redundant material – words not needed to work out the answers – provides you with a breather, if you can recognise it, e.g. *Einige Artikel sind heute Sonderangebote.*
1 If you did not catch *Sportartikel*, the mention of *die neuen Hemden von Bayern München* (famous German football team) might alert you.
3 If you missed *Kleidung*, the description *die neueste Mode aus Paris* tells you it is about clothes.

Task		Answer	Mark
E	1	B	1
	2	A	1
	3	C	1
	4	A	1
	5	C	1

Examiner's tip   **1** The key word is *Flasche*.
2 You can ignore *Weiß-*. You need only catch *Wein*.
4 Clue: *ich habe jetzt keinen Hunger* = I'm not hungry now.
5 You need to understand numbers in prices. Here the word *Mark* comes in between two numbers, helping you to separate them. Try not to make the common mistake of getting them backwards (as in the wrong answer A)!

Task		Answer	Mark
F	1	15	1
	2	O/Keine	1
	3	C	1

Examiner's tip   **1** Don't just pick out a number you hear. He is not 16 until next week.
2 Don't forget that *Geschwister* means 'brothers and sisters'. Key: *Einzelkind* = only child; but the word *Nein* is enough to give you the answer.
3 Hopefully you heard the negative *keinen* before the word *Hund*.

Listening answers

Task	Answer	Mark
G	B	1
	D	1
	E	1
	G	1

> **Examiner's tip**
> In this kind of task, the pictures are usually placed in the same sequence as the corresponding mentions on the recording. Roughly half of the pictures would be incorrect answers to the task, as with Inge's hobbies here. The negative expressions help you to eliminate the wrong answers: A – *überhaupt nicht*; C – *keinen (Fernseher)*; F – *nie* = never.
> If you chose answer H, you confused *Schade!* ('What a pity!') with the word for 'chess' *(Schach)*.

Task	Answer	Mark
H 1	interessant	1
2	schwierig	1
3	schwierig	1
4	leicht	1
5	macht Spaß	1
6	nützlich	1
7	anstrengend	1
8	gut für die Gesundheit	1
9	langweilig	1
10	keine Aussage	1

> **Examiner's tip**
> *spannend*, thrilling/exciting; *nützlich*, useful; *keine Aussage*, no comment made; *anstrengend*, tiring.
> **1** *interessant* – an easy starter, because you hear this actually said. The remaining answers cannot be literally transferred from the recording but need to be worked out.
> **2/3** note once more the importance of a negative expression – *nie* and *überhaupt nicht*.
> **2** *sich erinnern an* = to remember.
> **3** *Ich kann ihn nicht ausstehen* = I can't stand him. Note that questions might have identical answers when you are choosing from a more limited range of words, but this is unlikely to happen often.
> **8** Did you miss *keinen* before *großen*?
> *der Körper* = the body; *nötig* = necessary

Listening answers

Task		Answer	Mark
I	1	Brigitte	1
	2	Niemand	1
	3	Angelika	1
	4	Stefan	1
	5	Kurt	1
	6	Niemand	1

Examiner's tip *Niemand* = nobody.
There are six types of book and only four people. Two people might mention two types of book, but it is likely that at least one type of book will not be mentioned by anybody, in which case you will put a cross in the *niemand* column. The names of the people across the page on the Task sheet come in the order you will hear the people, but the books do not follow the order on the recording.
1 *sich verlieben in* (+ accusative), to fall in love with;
gut aussehen, to be good-looking.
3 *begeistern*, to inspire; *der Mörder*, murderer.
4 *eine Trauminsel*, an island paradise; *alles Unglaubliche*, all kinds of unbelievable things.
5 *die Umwelt*, environment; *faszinierend*, fascinating; *schützen*, to protect.

Task		Answer	Mark
J	1	Ja	1
	2	Nein	1
	3	Nein	1
	4	Ja	1
	5	Nein	1
	6	Ja	1
	7	Nein	1
	8	Ja	1

Examiner's tip There may not always be an equal number of *Ja* and *Nein* answers, so it's no good assuming that one half will be right and the other wrong.
2 The statement on the paper says that his parents leave him in peace, whereas you heard: '*meine Eltern fragen mich immer wieder*' – *immer wieder* = over and over again.
3 *Es ist ihm egal* = he is not bothered, but he actually said: '*Das ist es, was mich selbst ärgert*' – *ärgern* = to annoy.
5 His words were: '*Ich weiß noch nicht einmal, ob ich an einer Universität studieren will*' – *ob* = whether.
6 He likes playing the piano – *Ich spiele gern Klavier*.
8 He finds it silly that everybody wants to make as much money as possible: *Daß jeder möglichst viel Geld verdienen will, finde ich auch ziemlich blöd*. He adds that it is sad that money plays such an important part. However, he then says that he does not want to have financial worries, *finanzielle Sorgen*, that he buys only Levi jeans and dreams of driving a Mercedes, so he is also attracted by money!

Listening answers

Task	Answer	Mark
K	(a) It was difficult (to get used to driving on the left) (1) AND He got used to it/it got easier after a while (1).	2
	(b) He got into the wrong side of the car/taxi.	1
	(c) It (the public transport system) is better (than in Germany) (1) AND It is cheaper (1).	2

Examiner's tip
This exercise tests whether you can identify important points, themes and attitudes, draw conclusions, and make inferences.
(a) 'He had to drive on the left' is an insufficient answer. The question is about his driving, not about driving in England in general. Read the question carefully!
(b) You need to unravel a whole sentence with two subordinate clauses, rather than snatch at individual words.
(c) Did you misread the question? Many candidates fail here by giving the points against, of which there are many. Be patient and sift out the correct material. Some points seem favourable, e.g. *Sauberkeit*, but are negated by the rest of the sentence: *ließ zu wünschen übrig*.
The vocabulary required for the correct answers is not unduly hard, but it is a matter of detecting it on the recording.

L	1	Gestern um Mitternacht	1
	2	durch das Fenster (1) in der Küche (1)	2
	3	(Alter:) um die dreißig Jahre	1
		(Kleidung:) langer dunkler Mantel ODER Mantel und Mütze	1
	4	Er hat einen (richtigen) Schrecken bekommen/er war erschrocken (1) Er war nervös/nervöser als Frau Buchholz (1)	2
	5	Nach einer Viertelstunde/nach 15 Minuten	1
	6	(Er ist) zum Polizeirevier gefahren/mitgenommen worden	1

Examiner's tip
You are asked to write notes *(Notizen)*, not full sentences, so you can mostly get away without using a main verb.
1 Note the word *genau* in the question, so you need both details given in the answer for the mark.
2 Pay attention to the mark indication: two points are required.
3 Alter: *um die dreißig Jahre* = around thirty. 'Thirty' on its own is inaccurate – you would not expect to succeed with such an easy answer at Higher level. Kleidung: try to give as much relevant detail as you can in the space available. You would help the police more by describing the coat or by mentioning the hat as well.
4 *Schrecken* = shock. Again remember to give two details.
6 *das Polizeirevier* = police station

Listening answers

Task		Answer	Mark
M 1	(a)	Sunday	1
	(b)	Gave her/put on her a funny/cheerful/party hat.	1
	(c)	She was uncertain/doubtful (about the hat).	1
	(d)	Lots of people/everybody/most of the town/ whole town.	1
2	(e)	(They have built) a pedestrian zone/precinct/ it has been pedestrianised/cut off from traffic.	1
	(f)	That people took part/joined in. (*Played – incorrect answer*)	1
	(g)	It was real/genuine OR it was a folk/people's/traditional festival.	1
	(h)	A	1

> **Examiner's tip**
>
> **1(a)** If you mentioned Monday, you missed *vor* again: *am Sonntag vor Rosenmontag*.
> **1(b)** You have to describe the hat correctly for the mark.
> **1(d)** Did you hear *Männer* = men, instead of *Menge*?
> **2(e)** Be careful how you word answers, especially to the more difficult questions at Higher level. If you put 'No pedestrian zone' thinking it means there was no zone before, you have not made it clear: it could mean there is none now. A short answer is acceptable only if it is sufficient.
> **2(f)** If you missed the separable prefix *mit* you had the wrong verb: listen for *die Leute spielen hier richtig mit*.
> **2(g)** Did you miss the negative *nicht nur im Fernsehen*?

Reading answers

READING ANSWERS

Task		Answer	Mark
A	1	12.00	1
	2	11.00	1
	3	9.40	1
	4	8.50	1
	5	13.00	1
	6	8.00	1

> **Examiner's tip** In matching exercises, there will be some spare items which will not match up. There is only one here. You do not always have to read the whole text and understand all of the words in order to find the answers. If you know the words in the column next to the times you can immediately work out 4/5/6.
>
> You will notice that it pays in a matching exercise to start with the questions you can do easily, even if these are not the first ones. Then you can work on the remainder with a narrower choice: after doing the last three questions, the only times left are: 9.40/10.30/11.00/12.00.
>
> You could probably guess that your friend might be in the dining room/canteen at lunch time *(Mittagspause)*, and the mention of *Gulasch* confirms this = 1. You can eliminate 10.30 because the school yard *(Schulhof)*, given in the text, does not appear in the possible answers. You are left only with 11.00 and 9.40. You ought to understand *Bücher zurückgeben* (= returning books) to do 2. The remaining time of 9.40 has therefore to fit 3.

B

Teil A

	1	C	1
	2	E	1
	3	A	1
	4	F	1
	5	B	1
	6	H	1
	7	D	1

Teil B

	8	L	1
	9	N	1
	10	Q	1
	11	J	1
	12	R	1
	13	O	1

Reading answers

Task	Answer	Mark

> **Examiner's tip** Having done *Teil A*, you realise that there will obviously be some programmes left over, in other words some spare letters. The programmes in the answers will not come in the same order as they appear in the TV magazine. Like the lessons in Task A, they are jumbled up for you to sort out.
> This is a straightforward exercise in working out synonyms, or words with the same meaning or conveying the same idea, e.g.:
> 1 = Cartoons – *Zeichentrickfilm*; 2 = nicht krank – *Gesund(heit)*;
> 4 = Computer – *Informatik*; 5 = Kinder – *die Kleinen*.

C 1	(a) Thomas	1
	(c) Yvonne	1
	(d) Nina	1
	(f) Jochen	1
	(b/e) *These boxes should be left blank.*	
2	(b) Nina	1
	(c) Jochen	1
	(d) Thomas	1
	(f) Yvonne	1
	(a/e) *These boxes should be left blank.*	

> **Examiner's tip** You are being tested here on your ability to scan the texts in order to pick out the key words for the hobbies or the other statements. If you put a name in a blank box (**1b** or **e/2a** or **e**), you will lose a mark each time you do so. If you tick all 6 boxes for **1** or **2**, you will score only 2 marks (4 – 2 = 2).

D 1	B	1
2	C + E	2
3	B	1
4	D	1

> **Examiner's tip** 1 Do not select a number at random from the text. All the possible wrong answers on offer actually appear at the beginning of the passage. The correct answer does not! You can easily arrive at it by adding the number of boys (two) to the number of girls (one).
> 2 Be careful. The question asks what the family still has (in working order): only an old fridge and a new cooker.
> 3 The husband may have mended the washing machine a few times, but he did not enjoy doing it: *das hat ihm keinen Spaß gemacht*.
> 4 You have to understand the husband's suggestion that the washing can be done by hand, *mit der Hand*, then the woman's order to her husband, *Dann kannst du die Wäsche selber waschen!* = 'you can do the washing yourself', and finally the fact that he agrees to do so: *Das tu' ich*.

Reading answers

Task		Answer	Mark
E	1	zu Ostern	1
	2	ist nicht ganz sicher	1
	3	ist nicht so gut in Mathe	1
	4	sind gegen	1
	5	als Koch arbeiten	1

> **Examiner's tip**
> 1 First notice the date on which the letter was written (*den 1.Mai*), then spot *letzten Monat* (i.e. April) in the second line. Sabine mentions that the weather in Germany at Easter was not as good as that which she sees on Kathy's holiday photographs (by inference from lines 2–3).
> 2 Clue: *weiß noch nicht ganz...* The words *nicht ganz* are more useful to you than *weiß* which could prompt you to choose the first (wrong) answer offered.
> 4 Don't go for the third answer offered because it matches the words *den ganzen Tag am Computer spielen* in the letter. Sabine's parents disapprove of this: *Meine Eltern finden Computer nicht gut.*
> 5 There is no mention of living in France and Jürgen finds languages difficult. The clues are a) that he is studying *Kochen*, and b) the words *als Koch* indicating his chosen career in the last sentence.

Task			Answer	Mark
F	1		getrennt (lebend)	1
	2		(a) 1 (b) 1	1
	3		Sekretärin	1
	4	(a)	'Misses Germany'	1
		(b)	schönste Ehefrau Deutschlands/schönste deutsche Frau, die geheiratet hat	1
	5	(a)	Musik (1); (b) Malen (1); (c) Reiten (1)	3
	6		ANY THREE OF:	
			Reise durch Deutschland (1) Modell sein (1)	
			in Fernseh- und Radiosendungen zu Gast sein (1)	
			beim Bundespräsidenten zu Gast sein (1)	3

> **Examiner's tip**
> When you have to fill in a form, a chart or a table you need to write only a word or a few words and not full sentences. The words you need are mostly to be found in the text, but you have to know where to look for them. To find them, you will have to understand the question and the text.
> 1 You have to work from the noun *Trennung* = separation.
> 2 *Zahl* = number; (a) can be worked from *Tochter*, (b) from *ihr Bruder*.
> 4(a/b) You have to have married to be eligible for this beauty contest. In English the title would be 'Mrs Germany'.
> 5 *musizieren* = to play a musical instrument.
> 6 *Ich habe vor* = to intend/plan; this indicates the future, as do *werde ... sein* and the modal verb *will*.

Reading answers

Task		Answer	Mark
G	1	Nein	1
	2	Ja	1
	3	Ja	1
	4	Nein	1
	5	Ja	1
	6	Nein	1

Examiner's tip
1 He only thought he was ill: *Er hielt sich für schwerkrank*.
2 Clue lies in his mother's question: *Aber wie sollen wir dich denn verstehen?* = How are we supposed to understand you?
3 Easier if you got 2 right: he says his friends are the same as his parents. Otherwise you can find the answer in: *Mit wem kann man schon reden?... Ihr bleibt alle stumm* = Who on earth can one talk to?... You all say nothing.
4 Don't overlook: *Das war alles nur Theater*, meaning it was all an act he was putting on.
5 Clue: *Ich weiß nicht, wo ich da anfangen soll* = I don't know where to begin. Note once more the importance of knowing synonyms: *beginnen/anfangen*.
6 See his reply to his mother about history: *Das ist ganz ohne Interesse*. The exclamation *Ach was!* is useful to recognise for Listening and Reading. Even if you don't understand what comes after it, you know that it strongly disagrees with the statement which came before it, here the idea of revising history.

Task		Answer	Mark
H	TEIL A	The correct sequence is b, d, a, e, c.	5
	TEIL B	The correct answer is d.	1

Examiner's tip
Part A: It is easy to lose a few marks by jumbling up the sequence. Answers can be found in the following paragraphs: b=1, d/a=2, e/c=4.
Part B: The clue is in the longest paragraph (3) which you did not need for Part A.

Task		Answer	Mark
I	1	Falsch	1
	2	Keine Aussage	1
	3	Falsch	1
	4	Richtig	1
	5	Richtig	1
	6	Keine Aussage	1
	7	Richtig	1
	8	Falsch	1

Reading answers

Task	Answer	Mark

Examiner's tip

General vocabulary:
das Treppengeländer = banister;
fiel... in die Tiefe = fell (a long way) down;
kopfüber = headfirst/headlong;
blaue Flecken = bruises.

1 Make sure you read the whole statement carefully, before deciding whether it is true or false.
2 There is no mention in the text of anybody cleaning or polishing *(putzen)* the banister. You should not have answered without looking carefully at this verb in the statement.
3 It was only later that the neighbour found him: *einige Minuten später*.
4 *sah Michael tot aus* = Michael looked (to be) dead. You should know *aussehen*, 'to look', and *scheinen*, 'to appear/seem'.
5 *der Rettungsdienst* = emergency/rescue service. Note also that another word for an ambulance is *der Rettungswagen*.
6 The policeman listens but says nothing!
7 *etwas sein lassen* = not to do something; *verboten* = forbidden.

J	1	B	1
	2	D	1
	3	B	1
	4	D	1
	5	A	1
	6	C	1
	7	C	1
	8	D	1

Examiner's tip

1 As in Task D, do not pick out random numbers. You have to read: *Als er geboren wurde* and then link this with *Das war vor 13 Jahren* = that was 13 years ago.
2 You can eliminate answer B with *Tochter* and C with *seine Tante*. His aunt mentions that Heinz's mother has no friends, but that the boy does have one, so answer A is also wrong.
3 Eliminate answer A by spotting *kein* in the text. Heinz wanted to go to town (C), but his mother took him back home. For D, note *sich im Büro krank melden* means 'to tell the office that you are sick'.
4 A and C are what Heinz wants to be but is clearly not! For correct answer D, note *schlagen* = to beat up.
5 Cross out B by finding *nie* = never in the passage. Answer C is wrong, because he doesn't want his friends to play with him: *er will nicht, daß seine Freunde mitspielen*. There is no mention of D in the text.
6 A is what his mother thinks after Heinz has had a good meal, and B is what his aunt says children ought to do. Now that you know *nie* (from 5B), you can strike out D.
7 There is no mention of a job (A) in the passage.
8 B is contradicted in the story by *er redet kaum noch* = he scarcely/hardly talks. He bangs his door shut: *Er schlägt seine Zimmertür zu*, so C is wrong. This leaves only D, where *laut aufdrehen* means 'to turn up loud'.

Reading answers

Task		Answer	Mark
K 1	(i)	Um neugepflanzte Bäume zu begießen (1)	
	(ii)	Um sich die Hände zu waschen (1)	2
2		in die Forstschule	1
3		einen Traktor (1)	
		um im Wald aufzuräumen (1)	2
4	(a)	Sie kontrollieren (ODER reparieren) Nester.	1
	(b)	Sie bauen Futterhäuschen	1
5		Für Sport ODER Musik	1
6		daß er 75 sei/ist	1
7		(sie haben) die Natur geschützt/sie sind schon in der Waldjugend gewesen (1)	
		in derselben Gruppe/sie waren mit Klaus Huber/ Klaus war ihr Leiter (1)	2

Examiner's tip 1 You could get away with answering this by copying out the two sentences in the text which begin: *Mit dem Inhalt der Wagen...* and *Dann wuschen sich die Kinder...* Beware of copying chunks of the text, unless you are sure they contain clear answers. It is also quicker to put it in your own words, if you are able to, as you see in the model answer above.
3 Answer lies in sentence starting: *Nach den Gruppenstunden...* The second part of the answer *(Wozu?)* comes in the text before the first part *(Was?)*.
4 Easy if you learnt the seasons: *Frühling* = Spring, *Herbst* = autumn.
6 The remark after his age is your clue: *aber das glaubt ihm keiner* = nobody believes him.
7 You have to understand the final sentence by recognising the genitive plural of the relative pronoun *deren* = whose, and the verb which is placed at the end, *erleben lernen* = to learn to experience.

Task	Answer	Mark
L 1	Anna und Ogi	2
2	Marc	1
3	Nicole	1
4	Suzanne	1
5	Nicole und Kerstin	2
6	Verena	1
7	Kerstin	1

Examiner's tip If a text contains a number of names which you will need to answer the questions, it will save time to read the text carefully first, trying to remember the details about each person. Then take each question one by one, and you should find that you can answer some without having to re-read the details of each person for every question.
3 Nicole's parents treat her sometimes as a grown-up, but at other times like a child.
4 Contrast Suzanne's relationship with her parents at the age of 14 with that of today.
6 Verena wants to do things on her own and be independent.
See now if you can apply to Task M the skills which you learnt in carrying out this task.

Reading answers

Task	Answer	Mark
M 1	Judith	1
2	Merle	1
3	Judith	1
4	Peter and Merle	1
5	Stefan	1
6	Peter	1
7	Judith	1
8	Judith	1

Examiner's tip You have to read the extracts about the four teenagers before answering the questions. They do not follow the order of the text.
2 Clue: *Bei mir ist das Geld immer sofort weg*.
3 Although Judith speaks in the conditional tense about going to France, she also says *die netten Leute besuchen, die ich dort kennengelernt habe*, meaning that she has met them in France.
4 In this type of task you cannot rule out the possibility that more than one person is targeted by the question, and so you need to check each person for each question, unless you have a rapid memory. You will also note from the other questions that one of the four names is often the answer.
6 Clue: *auswandern* = to emigrate, go to live in another country.
7 Judith's parents only buy her essential clothes *nur Kleidung, die ich unbedingt brauche*. She spends money on the others (*Klamotten* = clothes).
8 Stefan is not the answer, because he buys presents for people.

N 1	a + b + c	3
2	b	1
3	a + c	2
4	b + c	2
5–12	The following should be ticked: 6, 7, 11, 12.	4

Examiner's tip For each box you tick above 12 you lose a mark (See Task C).
1 You must read the first three paragraphs to realise that all three statements are correct.
2 If you have read thoroughly while answering **1**, you will have spotted **b** in para. 2: *Wir haben... nicht so viel Geld*.
3 You will also have noticed **a** and **c** in para. 3.
4 See the first sentence of para. 5.
5–12 These statements refer to Frau Baumgartner's letter in reply to Anke's.
8–9 Frau Baumgartner suggests that Anke asks the Headteacher if the school could give her the money for the exchange, so these statements are incorrect.
10/12 The idea is that Anke's parents could ring Frau Baumgartner, not Anke's form teacher.

Answers to mock examination paper

MOCK EXAMINATION PAPER ANSWERS

Task	Answer	Mark

Note that the paper conforms to the new German spelling rules.

1

	bath	shower	TV	restaurant	parking	Stadtmitte
Waldheim	✔		✔	✔	✔	
Fischer		✔	✔	✔		✔
Sonnenberg	✔		✔		✔	
Eckert				✔		✔
Krone			✔	✔	✔	

6

> **Examiner's tip** Working total: 12 marks, one for each correct tick. From your total deduct a mark for each tick made in excess of 12. So, if you have 15 ticks and 12 are correct, you score only 9 (12 – 3). If you have 15 ticks and only 10 are correct, you score 7 (10 – 3). Divide this working total by 2 to give your final mark out of 6 (rounding up any half mark).

2	1	C	1
	2	E	1
	3	B	1
	4	A	1
3		The correct sentences are B, D, E (one mark each)	3
4		**1** F; **2** F; **3** R; **4** F; **5** F; **6** R; **7** R (F = Falsch; R = Richtig) (one mark each)	7
5	1	ein guter Junge	1
	2	aus dem Portemonnaie	1
	3	DM 20	1
	4	oft	1
	5	DM 35	1
	6	mit ihm reden	1
6	1	Sie ist nach Deutschland umgezogen/gekommen.	1
	2	(Sie fühlte sich) als Fremde/alles war ihr fremd.	1
	3	ANY TWO OF: (Darüber) dass Ausländer neben ihnen wohnten. Sie konnten die Fremden nicht verstehen. ihre Sitten/Gebräuche sind anders.	2
	4	Die (deutsche) Sprache/sie konnte nicht (gut) deutsch sprechen. (1) Sie war während der Pausen allein. Die Schülerinnen machten sich über sie lustig.	1 1 1

Answers to mock examination paper

Task	Answer	Mark
5	Sie ist Deutsche/sie akzeptieren sie als Deutsche.	1
6	Sie will in der Schule weiterlernen.	1
	auf der Uni studieren.	1
	einen guten Beruf erlernen/Anwältin	
	ODER Ärztin werden.	1
7	ANY TWO OF:	2
	Sie sind dagegen/gegen diese Pläne.	
	Sie soll zu Hause bleiben.	
	Sie muss ihre (kleineren) Geschwister versorgen.	
8	Sie machen ihnen Angst ODER sie sollen nur eine niedrigere Arbeit machen.	1

Examiner's tip When answering in your own German, you will have to manipulate the sentences you see.
You will often have to change the personal pronoun from first to third person:
1 *wir* to *sie* (singular – *die Familie* is followed by a singular verb form),
2 *ich* to *sie*, 3 *unsere* to *ihre*. You must turn subordinate clauses into a main clause with the verb in second position: Q5.

How did you do on the whole paper?

The paper covers the grades A* to D.

Grade A* = 37–40; Grade A = 33–36; Grade B = 29–32; Grade C = 25–28; Grade D = 21–24.

But remember that your final grade is based on all four components.

WRITING

To do well on this paper you will have to do the following:
Cover all aspects of the set questions. Tick off each sub-task as you do it, e.g.:
Question 1 *Gib Informationen über:*
deine Stadt/die nächste Stadt ✔
Question 2 – *Reaktionen der Fahrer* ✔ *und der Passanten* ✔
Remember in Q.1 that you are inviting your penfriend to come to stay with you and that you are also asking him a few questions.
Remember in Q.2 to make your report both clear and interesting. Note that you have to express feelings and opinions at this level.
High accuracy and a wide range of structures are required for the top grade.

SPEAKING

To do well on this paper you will have to do the following:
Question 1 Communicate clearly what is on your card and give a satisfactory answer to the unknown question (!).
Question 2 Convey the details in the picture and answer any other questions from the examiner using past tenses with reasonable fluency, accuracy and variety of language, and with good pronunciation.
Question 3 The same qualities are required as for Q.2 but present, future and conditional tenses should also be used. You should be able to take part in a genuine conversation. It is not enough to recite long passages of pre-learnt material. However, you should prepare sufficient material and try to say it aloud as practice, before asking a friend to examine you by interrupting you with questions.